DISCIPLINES
OF THE HUNGRY HEART

*Christian Living
Seven Days A Week*

R. Paul Stevens

Harold Shaw Publishers
Wheaton, Illinois

ISBN 0-87788-173-1

Cover design and illustration © 1993 by David LaPlaca

Library of Congress Cataloging-in-Publication Data

Stevens, R. Paul. 1937-
  Disciplines of the hungry heart : Christian living seven days a week / R. Paul Stevens.
    p.   cm.
  Includes bibliographical references.
  ISBN 0-87788-173-1
  1. Christian life—1960- I. Title.
BV4501.2.S7583   1993
248.4—dc20   92-42720
                                                        CIP

---

99 98 97 96 95 94 93

10 9 8 7 6 5 4 3 2 1

Contents

to
Carol and Stephen, Margot and Chris, David and Kathy—our children and their spouses.

Foreword

I am happy to write this foreword, for *Disciplines of the Hungry Heart* echoes my own conviction of the essential nature of the Christian life, as belonging to the "amateur status," when everything else around us is being so intensively professionalized. Masters degrees in friendship and Ph.Ds in motherhood are not far away from present living! So it is a pleasant assurance to have in this book the emphasis of the ordinariness of the Christian life. In fact, insistence upon religious *experience* is taking new conviction today, just as religious *feeling* had for many in the nineteenth century. William James reacted at the beginning of this century by claiming that true religious experience was limited to a few. Perhaps we may also need to react soon to the new openness that religious life is very ordinary experience for all.

Paul Stevens avoids this imbalance by reminding us that within the workaday world of seven days in the week, within which are set the relationships, disciplines, and actions of the Christian person, there is the added dimension of "the eighth day" that is transparent with spiritual life, indeed, by resurrection life. So implicit in every day and every week is the reality of the eternal that transcends the temporal, helping to purify the "ordinariness" of life with the spiritual reality of God's Holy Spirit that can indwell us.

This book is about the shaping and directing of Christian persons and thus not merely about making a profession out of description of the faith. It is a book that takes sides with Jesus, as he faced similar issues in his day: the legalism of

Judaism; the institutionalized self-interest; and the materialism around him that encumbered the worship of the true God. We are well aware how much we need a similar posture today, by uncovering the essential simplicity of the Christian life. But this requires also the humble and prayerful illumination of the commonplace, as it is also bathed in the presence of divine love. It is my prayer that this book will be read by many as a redirection for the despising of "ordinariness." May it help you, dear reader, immersed in life's complexities and temptations, to live an "Eastered life," of bringing the risen Christ into all of your humanness. It is what George Herbert meant by:

"Heaven in ordinarie, man well drest."

James M. Houston
Regent College

Mere Spirituality: An Introduction

"I believe in Christianity as I believe that the Sun has risen, not only because I see it but because by it I see everything else."—C. S. Lewis

Ever since I was first touched with the warmth of God's love I have been ambivalent about formalized, institutional Christianity as a religion. At the same time I have always been fascinated with Jesus and his love for life. I now welcome this ambiguity as a challenge to distinguish between the husk and the heart of true Christianity. The husk is the formalized religious apparatus for finding and pleasing God and for saying one's prayers correctly.[1] But the heart is the God-invasion of our seven-day week with transcendent meaning and irrepressible joy.

The Seamless Fabric of Faith

It has been said that the primary contribution the Hebrews made to religion was to do away with it! How much more has Jesus transcended religion by offering in himself the permanent irruption of his life into our lives, so making himself the Way. In this book I explore the spirituality of everyday life. Spirituality is about roots, about living deeply grounded, non-superficial lives, about the possibility of holiness for the ordinary Christian in the thick of life. To discover God where we are we must explore the relationship between hectic living and spiritual growth.[2] This will yield a spirituality that is neither monastic nor clerical, but rooted in homemaking, doing business, loving one's spouse, casting one's vote in the municipal election, and caring for the poor and powerless. Spirituality is simply communion with God. But for the biblical Christian this communion must be embodied, incarnated, and threaded into everyday, earthly realities.

Originally God intended everything to be bound and woven together in a single seamless fabric of faith, hope, and love. The Bible opens with a man and woman at work, forming a family and celebrating their sexuality. In due course their descendants began to call on the name of the Lord (Gen. 4:26) and became a family of promise and a microchurch, brothers and sisters in a family that transcended the ties of kith and kin. They experienced aloneness negatively as loneliness—Cain being the first restless wanderer (Gen. 4:14)—and positively as solitude—Enoch being the first true friend of God (Gen. 5:24).

Adam and Eve were awakened into consciousness to experience the seventh day, one day of rest to discover the meaning of the other six. So this book is crafted around the structure of the common ventures of a seven-day week in order to communicate that the Christian way is an everyday adventure and not merely the quest for spiritual ecstasy in retreat centers, monasteries, and sanctuaries. According to the New Testament, pleasing God has very little to do with church services, and everything to do with living our whole lives wholly for God (Luke 11:33-36). So the first day in our journey through a week in the life of the ordinary Christian will be spent exploring the spirituality of work. Work links us with the God who works.

Finding Meaning in Work

The Bible opens with God hard at work, crafting things and people. God scrapes up dust (which he has carefully made) and breathes into the molded clay (Gen. 2:7), imparting an artistic expression of himself: shaping, separating, speaking, and forming. The Bible ends with God still at work re-creating and transfiguring what he and his creatures have made—a city of exquisite beauty (Rev. 21–22). Apart from keeping the Sabbath, which turns out to be the meaning of both his work and ours, God never stops working. Neither does Jesus (John 5:17); nor should humankind, because work is not only our duty but our dignity.

I have just finished building a cedar deck for our cabin. It has a tempered glass perimeter so our grandchildren can safely push their noses to the glass while they look at the constantly changing sea below. An arbutus tree grows awkwardly through the middle of the deck exactly where a table would normally be placed. But the tree belongs, so we will sit around the tree. The day I finished building the deck, I repeatedly walked out the front door to view it from different angles. Over and over again I said to myself (and to God), "It is good! It is beautiful!" in an echo of God's satisfaction over his own labors (Gen. 1). I wondered if God enjoyed and appreciated my deck as much as I did. Simple satisfaction in a job well done can turn into egoism if not returned to God, but if it is returned to God it is multiplied into praise. So even something as mundane as building a deck can become an act of worship. In "A Day at Work" we will ask what makes work Christian. It is an important question.

The average North American person spends some 88,000 hours on the job from the first day of full-time employment until retirement. Work occupies about 40 percent of his or her waking life. In contrast, a dedicated Christian is estimated to spend as few as 4,000 hours in a lifetime in church meetings and church-related activities.[3] The church seems to have made spirituality into a leisure-time, discretionary-time involvement that provides a welcome relief from the boredom of work, or a challenge to the all-consuming demands of the marketplace. But true spirituality is more subversive than that. It sneaks into the center of our lives, compelling us to find God in the down-to-earth rather than the up-in-heaven. We have a down-to-earth God who went through the complete human experience from conception to resurrection. So to be Godlike people we must become equipped to work *for* God and to work *with* God. For both God and humankind are workers, and work is a powerful link between the Creator and his creating creatures.

Domestic Holiness

Just as prayer and work belong together, so do prayer and family life. The philosopher Alfred North Whitehead once said that religion is what we do with our solitariness.[4] Biblical spirituality is irrevocably relational and domestic. We have a social God who created us in his image as social beings (Gen. 1:27). We are neither created nor saved alone. God designed us to live in families formed by covenant, blood, or adoption. While the family has never before in history suffered such disintegrating forces as it does today, this fundamental reality remains: God is family, and every family in heaven and on earth derives its dignity from the social life within God himself: Father, Son, and Holy Spirit dwelling in a love community of belonging (Eph. 3:15).

So it was entirely appropriate that the second Vatican council used the phrase *domestic church*[5] to recapture the ancient idea that the family is a form of the church and a place for evoking and applying faith. Karl Rahner spoke of marriage as "the smallest . . . true community of the redeemed and the sanctified."[6] Implied in this is the idea that we do not need to bring the Lord "into" our homes by a program of Christian education for the family or even by family devotions, good as these are. God is already there. He has never left the family, whether the home is "good" or "not so good.["7] While there are no perfect families, there is no better family for us to be formed more fully into Christian maturity than the one in which we were born or adopted, or the one that we entered by the marriage covenant.

Prayer and Sexuality

The third "day" will explore our everyday experience of the opposite sex. God made us male and female in his image (Gen. 1:27) and inextricably linked our sexuality and our spirituality. This one truth ought to save us from either deifying or denigrating our sexuality. It should also provoke us to explore the relationship of sexuality and prayer, male and female spirituality, and gender partnership in spiritual ministry—matters we will take up in the section on "The Other Sex." Our sexual appetite is not a restless demon inside that must be sublimated and suppressed, if not fully exorcised, in order for a person to become holy and Christlike. The opposite is true: sexuality is the gracious call of God to find our true wholeness together with the other sex and not in isolation.

The word *sex* comes from the Latin *secare*, which means "to cut or to divide. Something has been separated that longs to be reunited." Thus, as Richard Rohr says so insightfully, "the power and energy of sexuality . . . is the power of the opposite and the energy of a certain kind of opposition." Sexuality reveals something at the very heart of reality and "is a constant expression of the Spirit."[8] He concludes that our search for sexual wholeness and our commitment to the life of the kingdom conspire to deepen our life in God, each contributing to the other interdependently. Our daily experience of the sexual corollary of life offers us one more path to God, one more opportunity to be contemplative, one more invitation to be prayerful. So does our day with our Christian brother and sister in the Lord's family.

Brothers and Sisters

When Jesus invites us to become his followers, he invites us to become his brothers or sisters, and members of the same family—siblings in the faith. But our Christian brother or sister is a real and not an ideal person, and visionary dreaming about Christian community will destroy fellowship.[9] Walter Hilton, the fourteenth-century Augustinian canon, once said, "It is a great victory for a person just to be able to love his fellow Christian in charity."[10]

"A Day with Brothers and Sisters" will explore the Christian's relational life under the rubric of priesthood, specifically the biblical doctrine of the priesthood of all believers. The bookshelves groan with books on spiritual gifts, worship, small group ministry, lay counseling, mutual pastoral care, and relational integrity. What we must do is get inside the relationships that comprise the family of God and allow these relationships to become mutually sacramental—a gracious touch of God to one another.

The Mixed Life

Connecting with our brothers and sisters is impossible unless we have the reflective experience of a day alone. Six centuries ago, Walter Hilton addressed this fundamental challenge in *Letters to a Layman*. The layman, apparently a man of affairs and important in commercial or political life in England, had a vital experience of the Holy Spirit and wanted to enter a religious community as a contemplative and abandon family, business, and friends. Walter Hilton recommended what he calls a third way.

The first way is the active life, in which a Christian is preoccupied with life in the secular world. The second is the contemplative life, which is a life exclusively dedicated to spiritual service in a religious community. But Walter Hilton advised embracing "the mixed life," which combines the activity of Martha with the reflectiveness of Mary.[11] So the day alone is set aside for the journey upward and the journey inward. The upward journey involves deepening our relationship with God through Bible meditation and solitude. The journey inward involves coming to terms with ourselves, walking around in the company of our own souls and allowing God to heal our emotional wounds. But these journeys lead naturally to the journey outward: love for one's neighbor.

The Neighbor As a Means of Grace

The biblical concept of neighbor transcends family, race, politics, culture, and geography. The neighbor is an important location of spirituality partly because the neighbor is uncontrollable.

> The neighbor bursts into everyone's life, outside the bounds of all provisions and beyond the scope of all planning. The great novelty of the Christian message is the duty to "prove oneself a neighbor" to others—the parable of the Good Samaritan. Neighbors cannot be chosen, but they are accepted at even the most inopportune moments.[12]

So we will consider three kinds of neighbors: the poor, the stranger, and the outsider. Each offers a challenge to show anonymous charity increasingly free of ulterior motives, even religious ones.

The neighbor becomes a means of grace precisely when the neighbor is taken seriously as a neighbor and not as a means of grace! We cannot simply deal with the poor, the stranger, and the outsider in principle, or engage in theoretical or strategic considerations of how to care for our global neighbors. It is in the context of actual neighbor relationships that we are invited to live the life of faith. Neighbor-love requires that we all become people-persons.

Sabbath Spirituality

Crucial for a spirituality of everyday life is the experience of the Sabbath. Sabbath is what our leisure-hungry and work-addicted culture desperately needs. The Latin American liberation theologian Gustavo Gutierrez writes about the need for prayer in this way: "Prayer is an experience of gratuity. This 'pointless' act, this 'squandered' time, reminds us that the Lord is beyond being categorized as useful or useless."[13] Sabbath *seems* to be a waste of time, but in reality it is the redemption of time.

The first mention of holiness in the Bible refers to time: "And God blessed the seventh day and made it holy" (Gen. 2:3). In contrast, humankind seems preoccupied with making holy *places*. Rabbi Abraham Heschel observes that all pantheistic religions are religions of space and sacred places, in contrast to the faith of Israel, which is concerned with the redemption of time.[14] The prophets maintained that the *Day* of the Lord was more important than the *house* of the Lord. In our culture, both religion and technology have been concerned primarily with the conquest of space. In the process we have forfeited experiencing holiness in time. Heschel says, "There is a realm of time where the goal is not to have but to be, not to own but to give, not to control but to share, not to subdue but to be in accord."[15] The great cathedrals, he maintains, are cathedrals in time. The Sabbath is the holy architecture of time. The meaning of Sabbath is precisely this: "Six days a week we live under the tyranny of things in space; on the Sabbath we try to become attuned to *holiness in time*. It is a day on which we are called upon to share what is eternal in time, to turn from the results of creation to the mystery of creation; from the world of creation to the creation of the world."[16]

Seven days. Seven ways of growing in Christ without abandoning work, family, and society. Seven dimensions of experiencing the fullness of the human condition "in both its natural and supernatural dimensions."[17] Seven contexts in which to live wholly for God and therefore to experience the biblical holiness.

Holy Worldliness and Worldly Holiness

Biblical holiness is a full-time matter. Kenneth Leech aptly states the need for an everyday spirituality:

> Today meditation and "spirituality" are being offered as commodities, as products of the social order, but as leisure-time activities which have no effect on society. Spirituality has become "privatized." . . . True spirituality is not . . . a diversion from life. It is essentially subversive, and the test of its genuineness is practical.[18]

If mysticism is simply a way of describing a direct awareness and relationship with God, experiential communion with God, then we are to become practical, seven-day-a-week mystics. Admittedly this is not easy in our secular society. The spirituality of everyday life must be "both worldly and unworldly."[19] We need both holy worldliness and worldly holiness.

Bonhoeffer expressed this in a conversation he reports he had with a young French pastor.

> We were asking ourselves quite simply what we wanted to do with our lives. He said that he would like to become a saint (and I think it's quite likely that he did become one). At the time I was very impressed, but I disagreed with him, and said, in effect, that I should like to learn to have faith. For a long time, I didn't realize the depth of the contrast. I thought I could acquire faith by training to live a holy life, or something like it. I discovered later, and I'm still discovering right up to this moment, that it is only by living completely in this world that one learns to have

faith. One must completely abandon any attempt to make something of oneself, whether it be a saint, or a converted sinner, or a churchman. . . . By this worldliness I mean living unreservedly in life's duties, problems, successes and failures, experiences and perplexities. In so doing we throw ourselves completely into the arms of God."[20]

We may throw ourselves into the arms of God and express ministry in the smallest things, like whistling while we walk or choosing a fresh approach during a conversation. It can be expressed in the way a letter is typed, or by the selection of a cartoon for the office door. Catherine Doherty speaks of "the holiness of little things done over and again for the love of God."[21] James Houston invites us to seek "guidance in prayer for every daily decision, every daily task, every smallest duty."[22]

The poet Blake spoke of seeing not *with* the eye but *through* it, thereby suggesting that if our perception were truly cleansed we would see everything the way it truly is— infinite.[23] Blake asked whether when we look at the sun we see a round disk of fire somewhat like a guinea. "O no, no," he said, "I see an innumerable company of the Heavenly host crying, 'Holy, Holy, Holy, is the Lord God Almighty.' I question not my corporeal or vegetative eye any more than I would question a window concerning a sight. *I look thro' it and not with it.*"[24] Our ministry in the ordinary things of life is to see *through* them to the God we love, thus making all life transparent to the glory of God, as Alfons Auer says, discovering "the sense of *transparency in worldly matters.*"[25]

PART ONE

A DAY AT WORK

"And now these three remain: faith, hope and love. But the greatest of these is love."
1 Corinthians 13:13

"We continually remember before our God and Father your work produced by faith, your labor prompted by love, and your endurance inspired by hope in our Lord Jesus Christ."
1 Thessalonians 1:3

1
Faith: Discovering the Soul of Work

"There is no work better than another to please God; to pour water, to wash dishes, to be a souter (cobbler), or an apostle, all are one, as touching the deed, to please God."—William Tyndale

"Do you like your new job?" It was a foolish question, a very Western question to ask a Kenyan. But Esther had been my student in a rural theological college in East Africa for three years. She had hoped upon graduation to be placed as a pastor of a church. Instead she was given the enormously demanding task of being matron for three hundred girls in a boarding school. It was a twenty-four-hours-a-day, seven-days-a-week job with little recognition and limited remuneration. So I had reason to ask. But her answer revealed a deep spirituality, one which I covet for Christians in my home country and for myself. She said, *"I like it in Jesus."*

Esther might have answered, "I am enduring it for Jesus' sake," or "It is not what I would have chosen but I am trying to accept it as 'my cross.' " But to "like it in Jesus" is the soul of work and the spiritual center to which Paul appealed when he affirmed the Thessalonians for their "work produced by faith, labor prompted by love, and endurance inspired by hope in our Lord Jesus Christ" (1 Thess. 1:3). Exploring working in faith, love, and hope will provide a spiritual understanding of work that is based on the Word of God. A sermon can be delivered for the devil's glory and a sweater knitted as a sacrament. Work is not merely salaried employment. And Christian work is not merely work that obviously directs people's attention to God. It is not the exterior form of the work that makes it Christian, but the interior of it—the spirituality of work.

The Uselessness of Work

One strange fact about the Word of God is that it sometimes asks a question rather than gives an answer. The question posed by the Professor in the Old Testament book of Ecclesiastes is probing and not rhetorical: "What does a man get for all the toil and anxious striving with which he labors under the sun?" (Eccles. 2:22). The inspired author himself is genuinely searching for an answer, and not merely exciting interest in the answer he is about to supply.

This question probes the depths of our experience of work. It is asked not only by people at the end of a long, hard day at the office or home and by workaholic professionals who have discovered that their exciting careers are mere vanity and emptiness—this we could understand. But it is also secretly asked by people in Christian service careers who wonder if their preaching, counseling, and leadership is, in the end, useless and to no avail. "What does a man get for all the toil and anxious striving with which he labors under the sun?" Yet it is crucial to observe from Ecclesiastes as a whole that the professor is not just down on life. He affirms that "a man can do nothing better than to eat and drink and find satisfaction in his work. This too, I see, is from the hand of God" (2:24). So the professor is in a bind, and so are we.

God's Word does not always come to us with packaged answers. Sometimes God lets us join an inspired author like this professor in the process of inspiration, as he revels in the satisfaction of houses, programs, and pleasures as king of Israel and simultaneously judges that all he has done is a wisp of smoke, an empty bubble. These are the same mixed feelings Christians have about work: It's a blessing from

God, but also a curse. Work brings great satisfaction and health because it takes us "out of ourselves," as Bonhoeffer once said.[1] And yet it too easily becomes the idol by which we measure our own dignity and establish a pseudo-identity, and the idol ultimately fails to deliver true significance because we were not made only for work.

The professor deepens the bind by telling us why he thinks work is meaningless. First, it is temporary ("under the sun," 2:22). Second, we will eventually be unappreciated ("I must leave them to the one who comes after me," 2:18). Third, you may give your best energies and most creative gifts to a job that may be taken over by a fool ("Who knows whether he will be a wise man or a fool?" 2:19). Fourth, you are certain to experience injustice in the workplace ("For a man may do his work with wisdom, knowledge and skill, and then he must leave all he owns to someone who has not worked for it," 2:21). Finally, one must simply work too hard ("What does a man get for all the toil and anxious striving?" 2:22). So work "under the sun" (a code phrase in this book) is impermanent, unappreciated, resultless, unfair, and seductive.

Surprisingly the professor does not counsel us to cope with this by dropping out and squeezing all the pleasure we can out of life, including our work life. His reason is breathtaking: he is convinced that *it is God's will* for work to be useless! And God speaking through this professor asks us to reflect on our experience of work because he wants to call us to faith in a God who has determined that work should be, in one sense, useless. There is more revelation and faith in this man's dark ponderings than in many Christian testimonies of get-rich-quick and exhortations to praise the Lord on the job.

Work As Evangelist

If work, even volunteer work in Christian service, proves to be meaningless, then we conclude that we were not made for work but for God. If the professor is right, then we will not find satisfaction in our work through faith in God (the current "Christian" work heresy); instead, we will find satisfaction in God through our experience of work. It is a subtle but telling distinction; it is the difference faith makes.

Paul counseled the Thessalonians that their and our labor must be performed in faith, hope, and love (1 Thess. 1:3). He also said our labor "in the Lord is not in vain" (1 Cor. 15:58). This is not saying that evangelism, edification, and other obviously Christian acts of service are the only meaningful forms of work, as an old poem is popularly interpreted to mean: "Only one life, 'twill soon be past; only what's done for Christ will last." But rather, it means that all work at home, factory, school, and office done in faith will last and have intrinsic meaning: "Only what's done for Christ will last." In contrast, much "Christian" work that is done to find meaning in the work itself, especially work that brings glory to ourselves, will in the end prove to be an empty and disappointing idol and will be burned along with the hay and stubble on the last day.

So this deep experience of resultlessness we share with the professor turns out to be an inspired frustration. His holy doubt gives us the opportunity to find in God what we cannot find in work. Work is an evangelist that directs us to Christ. And the gospel we hear from Jesus is not that if we accept him we will be insanely happy and successful in our jobs, but that we will find satisfaction in Jesus. He alone can fill the God-shaped vacuum in our souls. So it is not just the Old Testament professor but Jesus who asks this probing question. With absolute courtesy Jesus comes to us in the workplace not to tell us what to do with our lives, but to ask what we are discovering in our search for meaning in our work. And then, with infinite grace, he offers himself.[2]

Work is one context in which we meet, love, and serve God. Far from being a diversion from the spiritual life, work takes us directly to God through its creative possibilities and its purifying pressures. That is the soul of work. But now we must get inside the experience of working for Jesus.

Working for Jesus

The idea that Jesus is our boss is not a new one in Christian circles, but it is seldom understood. At a very preliminary level it means that we are ultimately accountable to Jesus for the stewardship of the gifts and talents he trusted us with. The Parable of the talents leads us at least that far (Matt. 25:14-30). It is a sin to squander what God has given us to use, or to wrap up our talents, our ideas, and our dreams in a handkerchief and bury them for fear of losing them through a risky experiment or by doing our work incorrectly. We are accountable. We may sympathize with the one-talent person, but we must always remember that the source of his conservatism was his inadequate view of God (Matt. 25:24-25). We have a God who wants us to take risks, and we are accountable for the risks we do not take!

But there is more than simple accountability involved in working for Jesus. It is sometimes suggested that we should treat our boss *as if he or she were Jesus,* and to do so on the authority of Ephesians 6:5. "Slaves, obey . . . just as you would obey Christ." But that turns out to be a game of let's-pretend, and the more difficult the boss is to work for, the harder the game is to play. "Your boss may be a real bear, but Jesus is fun to work for" may appeal to the self-fulfillment culture of North America, but it doesn't go as deep as the spirituality of my friend Esther in Africa. She *liked* her work and her boss, in Jesus.

Both the idlers Paul was dealing with in Thessalonica and today's workaholics want to *see* the results of their work. The Thessalonian idlers thought there was nothing worth doing until Jesus returned (2 Thess. 3:6-13), and therefore work in this world was deemed resultless. Workaholics want to see the results of their work because it is the measure of their own worth and the means of establishing their identity. But working in faith requires something more, something that will be invisible to the outsider and the onlooker. Working for Jesus is a secret, a mystery. Paul instructs the slaves at Colossae, "Slaves, obey your earthly masters in everything; and do it, not only when their eye is on you and to win their favor, but with sincerity of heart and reverence for the Lord. Whatever you do, work at it with all your heart, as working for the Lord, not for men, since you know that you will receive an inheritance from the Lord as a reward. It is the Lord Christ you are serving" (Col. 3:22-24).

There are three faith-secrets being kept here: first, Christians in their work are making a secret *appeal*—not to draw attention from onlookers or only when the supervisor is looking, which is ophthalmic service. Second, they have a secret *purpose*—to win favor not from other workers or their human bosses, but from God. And third, they have a secret *reward* in mind—not the paycheck but the anticipated inheritance from the Lord.

Jesus As the Recipient of Our Work

This passage from Colossians says that Jesus himself is the recipient of our work, as he is the recipient of all human behavior in his own body. That transcendent truth is visualized clearly in his representative and substitutionary suffering on the cross. But this is the wrinkle of faith: This reception of our service by Jesus happens in precisely those situations where *it was not apparent to us that Jesus was actually there*, when the visible results of our work were missing, when it did not appear that our efforts were a work of faith. That is the seldom-mentioned crucial point in the parable of the sheep and goats (Matt. 25:31-46). On the last day the righteous who are invited to possess their inheritance in the kingdom will find out that their service on earth was given directly to Jesus, who received their work as directed to himself. But they will not say, "I remember serving you, Jesus." Instead they ask, "When did we see you sick or in prison and go to visit you?" (verse 39). And the unrighteous are quite adamant that if they had seen Jesus himself in need they would gladly have served, for they say, "Lord, when did we see *you* hungry or thirsty or a stranger or needing clothes or sick or in prison, and did not help *you?*" (verse 44). Jesus replied that "whatever you did not do for one of the least of these, you did not do for me" (verse 45).

I leave aside the question of whether "these brothers of mine" (verse 40) refers to Christians in need or merely people. I cannot think it makes any difference. The implication of the parable is disturbing: Surprise is the litmus test as to whether there was faith in the original work. One of the goals of all spirituality is to set us up to be surprised by the seeking Father. While on this earth we spend our powers in the service of our neighbor through our daily work and our occasional acts of charity, "but in heaven," Wingren points out, "it is made evident that the poor neighbor whom we served was Christ, the King."[3] I believe that this is true whether our work is obvious service to our neighbors as expressed through the helping professions, or indirect service through those occupations that keep the fabric of the world stable, like garbage collectors, accountants, and telephone repair-persons. But the issue is this: How can we be set up to be surprised?

Personally, I find it unhelpful *to imagine* that the person or persons I am serving through my work is Jesus. I do not wish to denigrate the beautiful faith of Mother Teresa, who advises such a strategy of seeing Jesus as he comes to us disguised in the visage of his suffering, wounded, demanding, and hard-to-love brothers. But I find little scriptural warrant for believing that faith makes us "see" Jesus *instead of the person*. There would be no surprise on the last day if we had imagined ourselves doing everything for Jesus and to him. And there is a love reason for refusing this pretence.

Love demands that I take my neighbor with utter seriousness as he or she is, especially if that neighbor is my spouse, my boss, or my employee. No one wants to be loved by deflection, but rather to be loved as they are. Earlier I mentioned that our neighbor proves to be a means of grace precisely when he or she is not regarded as such, but regarded as a real neighbor! Working in faith means working without being able to see the results at the time.

Faith takes a different tack. By faith I believe *Jesus actually meets us* in the workplace or in an act of service in some way that I cannot control, predict, or see. And faith in Jesus allows me to decide that *my response to a person's needs or demands will be determined by Jesus and not by that person*. The bottom line is that we are doing it for Jesus, and not for the gains we will make by doing it "in faith." The goal is God, not our inheritance from God or even the joy of working. Attending to God himself—even more than the things of God—is the goal of true contemplation, especially contemplation in the marketplace.

So working in faith involves the total relinquishment of any attempt on our part to control the presence, the blessings, or the grace of God. It recognizes that we cannot generate ministry out of our daily work, even if that work is preaching or counseling. The man or woman who lives by faith has purposed that all of his or her life will be lived for God's glory and trusts God with his or her actions even when there is no obvious "ministry" attached to them— especially when he or she responds to a call for service or a request for work *that is not obviously a Christian service to Jesus*. Otherwise there would be no surprise on the last day. Sometimes we may be consciously ministering to Jesus (as Mother Teresa speaks about), but that is a gracious gift given from time to time, not a sacred necessity.

It is a sobering thought that the roles of so-called Christian workers are often chosen because the work can be obviously done for and to Jesus. Many people go "into the ministry" because it is apparently a direct way of serving God, without realizing that it is the indirect ways that are singled out for conspicuous faith on the final day of evaluation. It's not a sin to want to serve God in an obvious way, but it may not be work done in faith even though it was "Christian work." The Lord might say to me on that day: "Much of what you did in teaching and preaching, and even in your books, Paul, was obviously done for me, but let me tell you what you did in faith." And he will surprise me. I pray he will.

Calvin Seerveld tells a moving story from his childhood that illustrates the mystery of working in faith.

> My father is a seller of fish. We children know the business too having worked from childhood in the Great South Bay Fish Market, Patchogue, Long Island, New York, helping our father like a quiver full of arrows. It is a small store, and it smells like fish. I remember a Thursday afternoon long ago when my Dad was selling a large carp to a prosperous woman and it was a battle to convince her. "Is it fresh?" It fairly bristled with freshness, had just come in, but the game was part of the sale. They had gone over it anatomically together: the eyes were bright, the gills were in good colour, the flesh was firm, the belly was even spare and solid, the tail showed not much waste, the price was right. . . . Finally my Dad held up the fish behind the counter, "Beautiful, beautiful! Shall I clean it up?" And as she grudgingly assented, ruefully admiring the way the bargain had been struck, she said, "My, you certainly didn't miss your calling."
>
> Unwittingly she spoke the truth. My father is in full-time service for the Lord, prophet, priest and king in the fish business. And customers who come into the store sense it. Not that we always have the cheapest fish in town! Not

that there are no mistakes on a busy Friday morning! Not that there is no sin! But this: that little Great South Bay Fish Market, my father and two employees, is not only a clean, honest place where you can buy quality fish at a reasonable price with a smile, but there is a spirit in the store, a spirit of laughter, of fun, joy inside the buying and selling that strikes the observer pleasantly. . . . When I watch my Dad's hands— big beefy hands with broad stubby fingers each twice the thickness of mine, they could never play a piano—when I watch those hands delicately split the back of a mackerel . . . when I know those hands dressed and peddled fish from the handlebars of a bicycle in the grim 1930s . . . twinkling at work without complaint, past temptations, always in faith consecratedly cutting up fish before the face of the Lord—when I see that I know God's grace can come down to a man's hand and the flash of a scabby fish knife.[4]

2

Love: Recovering the Amateur Status of the Christian

"To discover God in the smallest and most ordinary things, as well as in the greatest, is to possess a rare and sublime faith. To find contentment in the present moment is to relish and adore the divine will in the succession of all the things to be done and suffered which make up the duty to the present moment."
—*Jean-Pierre De Caussaude*

"What you do in your house is worth as much as if you did it up in heaven for our Lord God."—*Martin Luther*

"Does God work?" Willie MacMichael asks his father in George MacDonald's book for children. His father answered biblically:

> "Yes, Willie, it seems to me that God works more than anybody—for He works all night and all day and, if I remember rightly, Jesus tells us somewhere that He works all Sunday too. If He were to stop working, everything would stop being. The sun would stop shining, and the moon and stars; the corn would stop growing; there would be no apples and gooseberries; your eyes would stop seeing; your ears would stop hearing; your fingers couldn't move an inch; and, worst of all your little heart would stop loving."

"No, Papa," cried Willie. "I shouldn't stop loving, I'm sure."

"Indeed you would, Willie."

"Not you and Mamma."

"Yes—you wouldn't love us any more than if you were asleep without dreaming."

"That would be dreadful."

"Yes, it would. So you see how good God is to us—to go on working, that we may be able to love each other."

"Then if God works like that all day long, it must be a fine thing to work," said Willie.

"You are right. It is a fine thing to work—the finest thing in the world, if it comes of love, as God's work does."

MacDonald ends with this insightful comment:

This conversation made Willie quite determined to learn to knit. If God worked, he would work too. And although the work he undertook was a very small work, it was like all God's great works; for every loop he made had a little love looped up in it, like an invisible, soft, downy lining to the stockings. And after those, he went on knitting a pair for his father, and learned to work with a needle as well, and to darn the stockings he had made.[1]

In its original meaning, *amateur* described the person who does something for love, but the word has come to mean unprofessional or unqualified—the opposite of *professional*. George Bernard Shaw once said that every profession is a conspiracy against the laity. In Christian ministry this conspiracy has dealt a fatal blow to the ministry of every member of the body of Christ since the tendency is to leave ministry to the paid professionals "who know how to do it better," while Christian ministry is essentially an *amateur* activity. In the marketplace, professionalism has robbed the worker of one of the strongest spiritual motivations to turn ordinary work into a sacred ministry, the motivation of love. What is work without love? Paul asks, "If I give all I possess to the poor, and surrender my body to the flames, but have not love, I gain nothing" (1 Cor. 13:3). If I burn myself out achieving professional excellence but have not love, my soul will be like a withered leaf, and my work will not touch people for God. When it comes to work there is something more excellent than excellence: love.

In secular society, identity is established by who you know, how much money you make, where you have been, and, most important of all, what you do for a living. To become unemployed is to face the ultimate identity crisis. But there is a better way to relate work and identity, the way of love. Walter Hilton expounds a statement attributed to Augustine and ultimately derived from the Gospels: "Man is naught else but his thoughts and his loves." So if we want to know who a person is, instead of asking what a person does, we have simply to ask what it is he loves and how he loves it.[2] Augustine and Jesus would make us amateurs and restore us to the genuinely human existence we enjoyed in the very beginning before sin marred our identity and our work.

The Prototype Amateurs

Adam and Eve needed no commandment to love God with all their heart, and their neighbor as themselves (Matt. 22:34-40). That law was written on their hearts, as natural to them as breathing. Within that single love vocation they were given three full-time expressions. Their first work is described rather than prescribed. Implicit in their humanity is the commission to work at *communion with God*. The first two chapters of Genesis describe the man and the woman experiencing the uninterrupted enjoyment of the presence of God in a relationship of loving awe. The text suggests that the garden was a sanctuary-garden and a place of real meeting with God.[3] No activity was intended to take them away from their center, though as in all relationships there were seasons of special intimacy, as suggested by God's walking in the garden in the cool of the day looking for his creatures' love (Gen. 3:8). Whether in laughter, which is an act of worship, or in naming the hippopotamus, Adam and Eve simultaneously celebrated their creatureliness and their God. The practice of the presence of God is not the exclusive vocation of professional ministers and cloistered monks because nothing on earth before the Fall should take us away from God. To make communion a part-time occupation is to make Christianity into another religion, perhaps not a very good one.

The second full-time work is also described but not prescribed. God's first negative statement in the Bible is that "it is not good for the man to be alone" (Gen. 2:18). In this figurative account of a literal event, God makes humankind innately social and inevitably sexual. "Male and female he created them" (Gen. 1:27). So *community building* is every person's second full-time job. Humankind is invited continuously to celebrate cohumanity, living in grateful awareness of the fact that neither male nor female can be the image of God alone, but only in relationships. This brings new meaning to the affirmation that "God is love" (1 John 4:8), for it expresses the symmetry of the relational life within God as Trinity and the relational life of his creatures. It also makes our sexuality contemplative. Each sex evokes the other's sexuality. Together they enable humanity to become a mysterious expression of God's own social experience and his covenant relationships (Eph. 5:32). The family becomes God's prototype community on earth and is part of every person's vocational calling, whether one remains single or gets married. People-making (Gen. 1:28) gives Adam and Eve the further privilege of making people in their own image (Gen. 5:3) as God made them in his.

So humankind's duty and destiny is to build community, to express neighborliness, to celebrate cohumanity—in a word, to love. We dare not relegate this to discretionary time activities. For example, it would be dangerous for me to think of myself as a part-time husband or a part-time grandfather. Some will earn their salary in community building by being town-planners or family counselors, just as others will earn it by prayer or evangelism. The way one earns one's living turns out to be incidental. The truth is that Christian vocation demands our all, all the time. The call of God that comes to every believer (Eph. 4:1) embraces all of life: work, family, neighborhood, politics, and congregation. We must never let our *occupations* become as all-consuming as our *vocation*.

Adam and Eve's third full-time job is *co-creativity*.[4] They were made regents, earthly rulers representing the interests of a heavenly king. They were to work not only *for* God but *with* God in making God's world work. They were made for the world, not the world for them (Gen. 2:5). The human task of cultivating and enculturating the earth included everything from farming to genetic engineering, from landscape architecture to playing the flute (Gen. 4:21). Eventually, Adam's children would do some of these things for a living. But, as I have said, that is incidental because earth-keeping is everyone's full-time job. But it will become an idolatry if it is separated from community-building and communion with God, just as preaching and other forms of traditional Christian service will become idolatrous if separated from homemaking and caring for the environment. So we were meant for the whole, not the part, and our health is in finding our down-to-earth God right where we are, in the business of ordinary life, doing our three full-time jobs and giving ourselves exclusively to none. This brings deeper meaning to the proposal that if we want to find out who we are, we need to ask who or what we love.

The Search for Lovable Work

When Paul wrote to the Thessalonians he did not affirm these Christians for "loving their work." Instead, he affirmed them for being people whose "labor [was] *prompted by love*" (1 Thess. 1:3, italics added), a much deeper thing. Not everyone loves his or her work, but love can turn even routine jobs into ministry by finding new ways to accomplish old tasks or incorporating the extra flair that love inspires.

Embellishment is one of the love-works that make the daily round interesting and, at least potentially, a ministry. As I write this I am perched in a guest house in a tiny Islamic village on the Indian ocean in Kenya. Most of the people are very, very poor, yet almost every wooden doorpost and lintel is rendered beautiful and interesting by exquisite Swahili carvings, each design unique. That required effort, the kind of effort love makes.

Falling out of love with one's work is like falling out of love with one's spouse: It is more of an excuse than an explanation. When people tell me they no longer love their spouse, I feel like telling them they are lazy. It is the same thing with work. If people cannot find some lovable dimensions in their daily work, it is often because they are expecting lovableness to be presented ready-made rather than discovered through prayer and hard work. Obviously there is no particular merit in staying in an unsatisfactory job if change is possible. And normally it is a good thing to search for a job that fits personal longings reasonably well (although half the world has no occupational choices at all). But I do not think any job, even one that initially seems to be a perfect fit, will sustain our love for long without spiritual effort on our part. Just as some people go from spouse to spouse looking for love, so others go from job to job looking for fulfilment. Normally we should find it right where we are.

While there are obviously some jobs that are not ways of loving our neighbors as ourselves, I think the list is shorter than some would imagine. Prostitutes and drug-pushers cannot love their neighbors in their work, but these are obvious examples, and it is socially acceptable to reject these. Much more complicated is the range of jobs in the "gray areas"—like a stock broker, or a collections agent who sells people's furniture from under them. Can these be done for love? Does the politician's work allow for love—or the work of a revolutionary, a soldier, an executioner, or an ambassador for a corrupt government? Someone working in the advertising field may be obliged, from time to time, to sell things by using sexual images. Can he or she work for this firm for love? An international buyer will find that success sometimes requires kickbacks, a complicated challenge that is viewed very differently in other cultures. Is there a place for love in such a business?

This pitiful list is enough to drive anyone to apply for the professional ministry. But there is no escape from the dilemma there either. Can a pastor be a minister of neighbor-love when the job description requires him or her to work in areas of personal weakness rather than strength? If a person does not love her work, can she still work for love? Some parachurch workers struggle when they are required by their mission organization to raise their own financial support. They feel they are compelled to "sell" their ministry to friends and family. Where is the love in that? A poorly paid professor in a Christian college is obliged to take on outside work because of his family's needs, but he does so for necessity, not love. There is no safe haven anywhere in the world or the church. Working for love is hard everywhere.

I dare say that no one works for love all the time. In all honesty, most of us live in a perpetual state of "sinning boldly but believing in Jesus more boldly still," as Luther would say. We live by grace and by practicing continuous repentance. But there are few jobs where the opportunity to love does not present itself. According to Luther, virtually all occupations are modes of "full-time" service to God except those of the usurer, the prostitute, and the monk.[5] In the same way virtually all occupations offer the possibility of loving service to other people. Some Christians are sustained day by day in the workplace by the thought that the product they are manufacturing meets a real need in the world. But some Christians are sustained by the thought that while the product they are manufacturing does not seem to meet a real need—it could be some trivial electronic device to complicate people's lives even further—there are people in the workplace they can love, or there are people at home who are receiving a loving benefit from their work. Unpaid home-makers are also working for love, sometimes *only* for love. This last point deserves some consideration because the Thessalonian church was having some problems getting some people to make the connection between work and love.

Love, Idleness, and Workaholism

Paul's shocking statement, "If a man will not work, he shall not eat" (2 Thess. 3:10) was made in the context of a church that expected Jesus to come back any moment. Some of them were thinking, *Why work, if the whole story will be consummated shortly and our work in this world will be rendered obsolete?* So they went from home to home living off the generosity of those who did work, instead of providing for themselves and their families as a loving act. Paul confronts this heretical practice by both example and teaching. He worked hard to look after himself and his companions as a love gift to the people he served. "We were not idle when we were with you, nor did we eat anyone's food without paying for it" (3:7-8)— a truly extraordinary statement from the lips of a traveling Christian worker. His teaching was equally radical: "Keep away from every brother who is idle" (3:6). In the same way Paul, in writing to the Ephesians, commands the thief to stop stealing and to work "that he may have something to share with those in need" (Eph. 4:28). One Christian reason to work is to make a love-provision for oneself and one's family. Viewed this way the idlers in Thessalonica were unloving. But, surprisingly, so are workaholics today.

Workaholics want to find their identity and fulfillment in only one of their three full-time jobs (communion, community-building, and co-creativity), whether it is mothering, administering, counseling, selling, or preaching. We were meant to experience a balanced life of living wholly and completely for God. But workaholics invest all their energies in one part of the human vocation, usually the "co-creativity" part in society. The reasons are well-documented. Usually raised in non-affirming environments, workaholics are attempting unconsciously to prove worthy of the approval of their parents and others. Workaholics are consumed by this inner drivenness and cannot play without feeling guilty. They have to work at play and cannot play at work. Work is too serious a matter. It often becomes misdirected worship as they use work to fill the God-shaped vacuum in their souls. A definition of idolatry is simply making something one's ultimate concern, other than the One who is ultimate. Even on vacations (if they take them at all) workaholics plan the next piece of work. Amos may be describing them when he rails against the people who spend their Sabbaths figuring out how to make more money as soon as it is over (Amos 8:5). The whole of life is oriented around what becomes one continuous work-week. But the outside effect of the workaholic is the same as that of the idler: *they are a burden* to all around them.

Workaholics have nothing to give because their love of work consumes all other loves. They require those around them to adjust their lives and priorities to the all-consuming nature of the workplace. Except for money they have nothing to give to those with whom they live: no affection, no joy, no friendship, no companionship, no love. They are emotional and relational thieves in the family and the community. So idlers and workaholics have some similar qualities when viewed from the outside—especially in their effect on others. But the inside comparison fares no better.

Both the idler and the workaholic are guilty of moral laziness.[6] Neither has gone deep enough to see that the reason to work as Christians is not simply for personal expression or to meet personal needs. *Work is a divine vocation*, a calling. As a vocation it is not something we choose as a way of finding fulfillment. Rather, it is out of response to a divine summons that includes our whole life: workplace, family, church, neighborhood and society. Ultimately it is God we must please in our work. And, to our surprise, we discover happily that God is easier to please than our parents, or even ourselves! So both the idler and the workaholic must become contemplative workers: true amateurs who allow the love of God to inspire their work.

The Much-Loved Worker

A passage written by Martin Luther is especially eloquent on this theme. Luther compares the love relationship between husband and wife and the love relationship between God and his children, a comparison that illuminates the spirituality of work and the amateur status of the Christian.

When a husband and wife really love each other, have pleasure in each other, and thoroughly believe in their love, who teaches them how they are to behave one to another, what they are to do or not to do, say or not to say, what they are to think? Confidence alone teaches them all this, and even more than is necessary. For such a man there is no distinction in works. He does the great and the important as gladly as the small and the unimportant, and vice versa. Moreover, he does them all in a glad, peaceful, and confident heart, and is an absolute willing companion to the woman. But where there is any doubt, he searches within himself for the best thing to do; then a distinction of works arises by which he imagines he may win favor. And yet he goes about it with a heavy heart and great disinclination. He is like a prisoner, more than half in despair and often makes a fool of himself. Thus a Christian man who lives in this confidence toward God knows all things, can do all things, ventures everything that needs to be done, and does everything gladly and willingly, not that he may gain merits and good works, but because it is a pleasure for him to please God in doing these things. He simply serves God with no thought of reward, content that his service pleases God. On the other hand, he who is not at one with God, or is in a state of doubt, worries and starts looking for ways and means to do enough and to influence God with his many good works.[7]

Christ himself must have experienced this freedom within love. During the so-called hidden years, he sanded and planed wooden cradles while he carried in his great heart the knowledge that the world was hell-bound. How could he have known what he knew and yet done such menial things in the carpenter's shop? Yet the Father said, "You are my Son, whom I love; with you I am well pleased" (Luke 3:22) when he had not yet preached a sermon or worked a miracle. This was probably not the first time God the Father assured Jesus of his love and thus liberated him to do little things for his pleasure before he went on to much bigger things.

3
Hope: Making Our Mark on Heaven

"The only ultimate disaster that can befall us, I have come to realize, is to feel ourselves to be at home here on earth."—Malcolm Muggeridge

"I desire to have both heaven and hell ever in my eye, while I stand on this isthmus of life, between these two boundless oceans; and I verily think the daily consideration of both highly becomes all men of reason and religion."—John Wesley

"If I knew that tomorrow the world would perish, I would still plant a little apple tree in my backyard."—Martin Luther

Years ago Lesslie Newbigin said, "We are without conviction about any worthwhile end to which the travail of history might lead."[1]

A few people believe we are heading into a new world order and paradise on earth, but most people nurse a deep foreboding about the future, or they try not to think about it. The seeming resultlessness of history even erodes the nerve of modern Christians, who have more reason to embrace the future wholeheartedly than anyone. Whether world-weariness and future fright come from the terrifying prospect of ecological doomsday, or from the conviction that Jesus will probably come back tomorrow, the result is the same for Christians: All work in this world except the so-called ministry is viewed as not very significant or enduring.

The old saying runs deep in our veins: "Only one life, 'twill soon be past; only what's done for Christ will last." The saying contains a deep truth, but it is popularly understood to mean that only overtly Christian work, such as evangelism or Bible teaching, will last. But Paul's affirmation of the endurance of the Thessalonians "inspired by hope in our Lord Jesus" (1 Thess. 1:3) concerned *all* work. So he said, "We command you, brothers, to keep away from every brother who is idle" (2 Thess. 3:6).

End-Times Idleness

Second Thessalonians 3:6-15 is one of the few New Testament passages on work, and Paul appears to be dealing with a problem completely irrelevant to modern Western nations, where workaholism is a way of life especially for professionals. Even the title in the *New International Version*, "Warning against Idleness," seems a dangerous challenge to people already killing themselves to become successful. But there is more to this passage than meets the eye.

Paul was confronted by people inoculated against work by the culture. In the Greek world work was a curse, an unmitigated evil; and to be out of work was a piece of singularly good fortune.[2] Unemployment allowed one to participate in the political domain and to enjoy the contemplative life. The whole of society was organized so that only a few could actualize the highest human potential. Work was called "unleisure." The Greeks had no sense of vocation. An individual's activity in society was called *ergon* or *ponos*, a burden and toil. During the fifth century before Christ, the government of Thebes issued a decree prohibiting its citizens from engaging in work![3] It was easy for Greek Christians to think of work as a curse, only partially redeemed by Jesus.[4] Better not to work if one could afford not to. How revolutionary it was for Christian slaves in such households to be told by Paul to serve their masters as though they were working for

Jesus (Col. 3:22-24)! How revolutionary for Paul to send home the runaway slave Onesimus, now converted and liberated, to serve his old master once again (Philemon)!

Further, in his ministry in the Gentile churches, Paul had to face a problem that is still with us. Instinctively when people become Christians they feel that the best way to serve God in gratitude would be to leave their "secular" jobs and "go into the ministry." Paul dealt with that by insisting that people can probably serve God best where they are: "Nevertheless, each one should retain the place in life that the Lord assigned to him and to which God has called him. . . . Each one should remain in the situation which he was in when God called him" (1 Cor. 7:17, 20). As Gordon Fee says,

> The two points Paul makes need to be heard anew. (1) Status of any kind (married, unmarried, slave or free) is ultimately irrelevant with God. . . . (2) Precisely because our lives are determined by God's call, not by our situation, we need to learn to continue there as those who are "before God." Paul's concern is not with change, one way or the other, but with "living out our calling" in whatever situation one is found.[5]

The New Testament treats work in the larger framework of the call of God to live totally for him and for his kingdom. All are called, and the call of God concerns all of one's life (Eph. 4:1–6:20). Therefore Paul, who earned his living by making tents, was not, strictly speaking, a bivocational missionary (meaning having two vocations—one secular, like tentmaking and one sacred, like church-planting). Paul was monovocational. He integrated his whole life of service as one passionate response to the all-embracing call of Jesus. There was no sacred/secular distinction for him.

But there was a further problem in Thessalonica—eschatological idleness. If Jesus might come back tomorrow, what is the point of working today? Missing the chance to work by faith, love, and hope, some believers wanted to "see" the results of their work, or they would not work at all. If their own projects would be "interrupted" by the imminent return of Jesus, why bother? They let others look after them as they moved from house to house absorbing Christian hospitality like sponges. Paul responded definitively: "If a man will not work, he shall not eat" (2 Thess. 3:10). Paul modeled what he taught, working night and day not to be a burden, and not eating food he had not paid for.

But having a strong sense of the end times need not incite us to abandon planning and pray for speedy evacuation. Just the reverse: Christian hope makes sense out of both short-term and long-term planning because we have a certain future in the coming kingdom of God. It can be argued that eschatology—the biblical doctrine about last things—is the most pastoral and helpful doctrine for the ordinary Christian to make sense out of the complicated everyday challenges of living and working in a world that will one day pass away. The last book of the Bible—the Revelation—is also a book about last things. It tells us how the world looks to a person in the Spirit. We see through the satanic seductions of society to the indomitable kingdom of God and join the multitude of heavenly beings who shout, "Hallelujah! For our Lord God Almighty reigns" (Rev. 19:6). The Christian has a worthwhile end to which the travail of history will lead. Being heavenly minded allows us to work on insoluble problems in the world with hope, but without being naively confident in our own efforts or burning out in discouragement while we try to make the perfect future happen. God's kingdom has come, and the kingdom is coming. That is the basis of the Christian's hope and the daily tension in which we live.

Ready for the Long Haul

It is claimed that Martin Luther once said that if he were sure Jesus would come tomorrow he would plant a tree today.[6]

This is totally in line with the parable Jesus told of the wise and foolish virgins. The only discernable difference between the wise and foolish virgins waiting for the wedding celebration is that the wise were ready for a long wait for the Lord to come again. Both the wise and the foolish wanted the Bridegroom to come soon. They both slept with impunity when there was a delay. But the wise virgins had enough oil for the long haul (Matt. 25:1-13). Believers are invited by faith to work today as though they had a long-term future, yet ready for the Lord to come at any moment. It is in this context that we can speak of the durability of our work in this world.

We are told in Scripture what will last until the end: "And now these three remain: faith, hope and love" (1 Cor. 13:13). John Haughey comments on this other occurrence of the triad of marketplace virtues.

> It seems that it is not acts of faith, hope and love in themselves that last, but rather works done in faith, hope and love: it is not the pure intention alone, nor is it faith, hope and love residing unexercised as three infused theological virtues in a person that last. What lasts is the action taken on these virtues, the praxis that flows from the intention, the works the virtues shape. These last![7]

Another passage that points to the same perspective is 1 Corinthians 15:58: "Therefore, my dear brothers, stand firm. Let nothing move you. Always give yourselves fully to the work of the Lord, because you know that your labor in the Lord is not in vain." Obviously Paul's first reference to "the work of the Lord" pointed to the various ministries engaged in by the Corinthian believers. But even these included such mundane things as "helping" and "administrating." In a larger application Paul is assuring his friends that what makes all their labor—whether homemaking or bridge-building—free from resultlessness is the fact that it is "in the Lord."

The Transfiguration of the Universe

Far from contributing to a hunger for instant evacuation, or a dichotomous approach to secular and sacred work, the New Testament invites us to explore the greatest hope imaginable for the world: Christ is Lord of Creation (Col. 1:15-23).

First Christ saves people, but eventually Christ will save all creation. This is the missing note in all environmental concerns—the note of redemption and hope. The oft-quoted landmark statement of Dr. Lynn White about the source of our environmental disaster goes partway, but not far enough. She says, "Since the roots of our trouble are so largely religious the remedy must also be religious."[8] If it is true that Jesus is Lord of Creation, then we must honor his intentions for the rest of Creation. Creation is not a commodity; it is not impersonal, but an artistic expression of the mind of God. Christ holds all Creation together. If as Bishop Lightfoot says Christ "impresses upon creation that unity and solidarity which makes it a cosmos instead of a chaos,"[9] we can say that creation is Christian.

Further, Romans 8:19-23 pictures a continuum of the present with the future in which creation "groans" for its consummation. As John Haughey puts it, "Creation's hopes will not be mocked by annihilation any more than ours will be."[10] The present will be factored into the future. The God who created with no materials will one day recompose the first creation with the materials of that creation over time including the work of human beings.[11] How this will be done is not told us, but we are invited to consider *which of our works will last* (1 Cor. 3:12-15). In view of the scope of re-creation envisioned, these works cannot simply be religious. Ironically, Paul envisions a situation in which the person's works are burned in the final fire, but the person himself is saved (1 Cor. 3:15). Perhaps many of my lectures and sermons will be burned like hay and stubble on the last day because they were judged not to be done for Jesus, while the deck I built, in some way that takes me beyond mere rationality, will survive the last judgment.

Making Our Mark on Heaven

It is apparent that through our daily work we leave our mark on the cosmos and our environment, on government, culture, neighborhoods, families, on the principalities and powers. The Bible hints that in some way beyond our imagination our marks are permanent. All the visions of the new heaven and the new earth are in terms of what we know and do now. The final vision of the Bible is one remarkably connected to our life now. "The kings of the earth will bring their splendor" (Rev. 21:24) into the New Jerusalem (a city we have known on earth) and "the glory and honor of the nations will be brought into it" (21:26). In one sense our environment is going to heaven. So is our culture, our government, our crafts, and our work.

The theological truth that undergirds this fascinating and challenging line of exploration is the statement that Christ is the firstborn of all creation (Col. 1:15) and firstborn from the grave (1:18). We have only to think of the resurrected body of Jesus to realize that there was a historical continuity between the body with which he walked in Palestine and the body that ascended to heaven. He was recognizable. And the most remarkable points of recognition for the apostles were the scars. His resurrected body bore scars in historical continuity with his life in the flesh, though the scars were not now merely signs of faith but had been transformed to become a means of faith for people like Thomas (John 20:27). They were transfigured along with the rest of his physical existence into something truly beautiful even though, remarkably, they were still scars. The resurrected body of Jesus is a powerful, evocative biblical symbol of the way this life is connected to the next life, especially as it relates to the physical environment.

Our violent acts against nature and culture may not be erased by the final Armageddon and the final consummation of the travail of history at the second coming of Jesus, but may by God's grace be transfigured. This is part of our hope. Through transcendent reasoning we can imagine that the marks we leave in this life and in this world last: open pit mines, well-manicured gardens, cedar decks, and satellite receiving stations, the good and the bad of what we are doing in this world. But there will be a transfiguration. There will be a *new* heaven and a *new* earth.

Work That Will Last

This brings new meaning to those whose toil is located in so-called secular work—in the arts, education, business, politics, the environment, and the home. Not only are ordinary Christians priests of Creation past and present; they, and not just missionaries, pastors, and Christian educators, are shaping the future of Creation in some limited way. Most Christians think that only religious work will not be in vain, but if Christ is the firstborn of all creation and the firstborn from the grave, then all work has eternal consequences, whether cleaning houses or being a stockbroker. Our hope is that we confidently look forward to a time of exquisite transfiguration. And the practical application of that hope is that we are invited in Christ to leave beautiful marks on Creation, on the environment, family, city, workplace, and nation. When we cannot do this and cannot undo the violence we have committed against the cosmos, we have faith in Jesus that one day he will transfigure even the environmental, social, cultural, and political scars we have left through our work.

"Only one life, 'twill soon be past; only what's done for Christ will last."

PART TWO

A DAY WITH THE FAMILY

4

Domestic Spirituality

"Home is the place where, when you have to go there they have to take you in."—Robert Frost, *in* Death of a Hired Hand

Robert Frost crafted this fascinating statement by a farmer whose old hired hand came home to die. The farmer resented the intrusion. Home, for him, was the place where someone *must* be taken in. But the farmer's wife had a deeper insight. She said, "I should have called it something you somehow haven't to deserve."[1] It points out a sublime truth. More than obligation is built into the structure of the human family. There is the possibility of grace, undeserved kindness. One does not need to go farther than one's front porch to be faced with gospel issues and to be found by God. Henri Nouwen calls solitude the furnace of transformation. But the heat is higher at home.

In his book *Finding God at Home* Ernest Boyer tells how he began to explore the liberating truth that family life *itself* is a spiritual discipline. At the end of a lecture on the spirituality of the desert—which involved leaving the comforts of family, friends, and homes to find God in the harsh Egyptian desert—Boyer asked the professor a probing question: "Is there child-care in the desert?" His journey—and mine—led to the conclusion that there is in a sense child-care in the desert in both the discovery of a personal spirituality in the context of family life and the discovery of a unique spirituality of the family.[2]

God designed the nitty-gritty of family life to "set us up" to meet, experience, and love him. For example, take this journal entry made by a mom in my home church.

Sunday. Up early making 150 cupcakes. An unexpected after-church guest. Ran out of sugar, fridge blew up—dripping ice cream announced its demise.

Monday. Repairman: "Have to send to Toronto for a part, should be here by next week." "Next week," I sputter. "What am I supposed to do without a fridge?" Repairman: "Sorry, lady, not my problem." Thank you, Lord, it was cold all week on the back porch!

Tuesday. Enjoying a quiet morning. Too quiet. Toddler develops new skill and escapes out of the front door and front gate—gone! Thank you, Lord, she wandered to a neighbor's house.

Wednesday. Trip to Cosco: two moms, two babies, three preschoolers—a mission destined for disaster! Stopped for diapers before Oak Street Bridge, only to be asked by the clerk: "Is that your van?" Thinking the children were screaming or hanging out, I fearfully said, "Yes." "It has a flat tire," the clerk replied. My heart fell. "O God, why today?"

My fellow adventurer quickly replied: "I know how to change a tire." I felt greatly supported. But where's the spare tire? Picture it: two moms, a crying baby, looking under the new van for the spare tire with the Automotive Manual in hand. "Now we've found the spare, where's the jack?" In the process, five men walked by, not one of them offering a word of encouragement or assistance. Reminded us of the Good Samaritan story. Ninety minutes later all was fixed. Thank you, Lord, it did not happen on the Oak Street Bridge.

That night a temperature and ear infection robbed Mom of sleep.

Thursday. My stiff neck became an "acute torticollis" as I put my neck out rescuing our baby from her sister loving her "to death." Help! I couldn't move. I felt fear. A few phone calls later, a friend answered, "I'll be right there." In ten minutes, with portable crib, baby and three-year-old, she came to my aid. There I sat on the couch, a bag of frozen peas on my neck, helpless, in pain, watching my friend clean my house, filled with appreciation and yet feeling humbled to be served and have my dirty house exposed. It is easier to serve than to be served. Thank you, Lord, for a loving friend. (I can still see her running around my house, Fantastik in hand, removing dirt marks.)

And my week goes on. "In thee, O Lord, will I put my trust."[3]

Family issues take us directly to God. But before we explore why, we must ask whether there is anything left that can be called family.

The Meltdown of the Family

Only a few years ago a Christian journal confidently asserted, "The family is virtually an indestructible institution which has prevailed in periods of tremendous stress and virtually impossible conditions."[4] No one could write that with confidence today.

Social commentators like John Conway in *The Canadian Family in Crisis* list the fundamental changes in family life today:

- In the 1990s one marriage in two will end in divorce.
- The duration of marriage before divorce has dropped dramatically.

- Fewer people are willing to take the emotional risk of getting married.
- Single-parent and common-law families are growing faster than traditional husband-wife families.
- Wife-beating and abuse—physical and sexual—are the fastest growing crimes across the country.
- Every year, tens of thousands of children suffer through their parents' marriage breakdown.[5]

The family has been attacked intellectually by thinkers like Kate Millett, who sees the family as the chief institution of patriarchy, and psychiatrist R. D. Laing, who views the family as a sick political arrangement or, more accurately, a protection racket.[6] Scientifically we are approaching the perfect contraceptive society, in which there will be no unwanted births. In a previous generation that would have eliminated most of us! Educationally, the family has been regarded as somewhat obsolete. Michael Novak makes this penetrating observation: "Education media help children become sophisticated about everything but the essentials: love, fidelity, childrearing, mutual help, care for parents and the elderly."[7] Culturally, the family is attacked through the reduction of its multifaceted roles (sheltering children, fulfilling legitimate sexual expression, providing emotional support, shaping identities, and providing a community of economic resources and benefits) to the one thing left for the family to do: meet emotional needs. When that is not done, many feel a moral obligation to leave home, or to leave an unfulfilling marriage. Michael Novak suggests there may be two kinds of people in this world: "individual people" and "family people." Sadly, he notes, the intellectual classes celebrate the former and denigrate the latter. Marriage seems a threat to the solitary individual.[8]

Sociologically, the family has suffered from profound social forces, some stemming from the Protestant Reformation.

Peter and Brigitte Berger consider Martin Luther the prototype of the autonomous individual. Protestantism fostered an austere individualism, and the family type related to this provided for the socialization of autonomous individuals.[9]

Probably never before in history have forces toward individualism been so rampant, and the family is suffering from this fragmentation. People now often insist on being called by their first names, while in older cultures the family name held their true identity. Indeed in Africa, until recently, the worst possible fate for a person was to be an individual, so strong is the family and tribal identity,[10] although this is rapidly breaking down through the global expansion of Western individualism.

Commenting on the demise of family, Michael Novak says, "In our society, of course, there is no need to become an adult. One may remain—one is exhorted daily to remain—a child forever. . . . In medieval paintings, children look like miniature adults. In tableaux from life today, adults appear as wrinkled adolescents."[11] Having children is no longer a welcome responsibility for, as Novak insightfully notes, "to have children is plainly, to cease being a child oneself."[12] The meltdown point has been reached. But stepping into the world of the Bible we find that family—in some form—is central to God's purposes, and Christians cannot stand idly by while society plans the dissolution of the family.

The Case for a Family Identity

When God wanted to create a community on earth in which he could dwell, he started with the microfamily of one husband and one wife: Adam and Eve. This formed the oldest community on earth. The family precedes the nation and the church. Later, to redeem the human race and to bless the nations he chose another family: Abraham, Sarah, and their descendants. Threaded through the story of the patriarchs is the truth that God will work with this family and promises never to leave them. He never did.

Much of the Old Testament legislation was family legislation and was concerned with family cohesion, family rituals, and family responsibilities. The family envisioned was much more extensive than the modern nuclear family. It included relatives, slaves (Deut. 15:12-18), and even alien immigrants (Deut. 10:19). In this context the Sabbath was a family day and a home festival, as were the Passover (Exod. 12:26) and Purim. As Eugene Fisher says, "In Judaism, the family is a religious worshipping institution. This is a major lesson Christians concerned for the family today can learn through dialogue with Jews."[13] The Talmud is rich in witness to the beauty and spiritual dignity of family life.

So the Old Testament and Judaism have left us with a rich inheritance of family life. But the picture is more complicated when we turn to the New Testament.

The Gospels record Jesus calling people to a higher loyalty than to father and mother, husband and wife, and children. While Jesus' family (Joseph, Mary, Jesus, and his siblings) is offered as a model (Luke 2:51-52), Jesus himself created a new community of disciples that crossed family lines, even his own, and offered himself as our brother in a new family (Mark 3:31-35). He envisioned that the radical call of the kingdom would bring division in some households (Matt. 10:21-22, 34-39), thus relativizing the claims of kith and kin. But believers would never be alone.

Jesus is the perfect model of a person who held together the claims of natural family and the family of God. At the wedding feast of Cana, Jesus found a way both to honor the request of his earthly mother (to work a needed miracle) and to obey his heavenly Father (by not disclosing himself prematurely) (John 2:1-11). At his crucifixion, while he was reconciling the world to God, he provided for his mother by arranging for her "adoption" into John's family (John 19:26-27). So both Jesus and his people belong to two families—one natural and one supernatural—and both are arenas of spiritual formation.

Further, the book of Acts describes whole families embracing the Christian way (Acts 16:34). The first churches met in homes (Rom. 16:3-5) and were really extended families. Paul uses family language to describe the church as the household of faith and "the family of believers" (Gal. 6:10). Ephesians 5:21-33 offers the highest possible view of Christian marriage: as an acted parable and divine mystery that links us with Christ and his church. It also offers a new political dynamic in the home: mutual submission (5:21)—the politics of grace. In harmony with many of the parables of Jesus about the messianic wedding feast (Matt. 9:15; 25:1; Mark 2:19) the final vision of the people of God in the last Bible book is a consummated marriage (2 Cor. 11:2; Rev. 19:7-9; 21:2; 22:17).

The New Testament letters contain rich teaching on family life. Of greatest significance is the teaching that God himself dwells in the inscrutable mystery called the Trinity, which, in some limited sense, may be spoken of as family. From his family every family in heaven and earth derives its name (Eph 3:15)—or derives its dignity and meaning. So family links us with God, *who is Family*.

On earth there are no perfect families, but there is no better family for us to be formed more fully into Christian maturity than the one in which we were born or adopted, or the one that we entered by the marriage covenant. Ray Anderson observes that

the relationships that place demands on our life through daily and domestic proximity determine to a large extent our spiritual formation, either negatively or positively. . . . Neither formal religious education nor spiritual exercises, either individual or corporate, can effectively replace or even overcome the lack of positive growth in these relations.[14]

No wonder the fifth commandment is the first one with a built-in promise (Eph. 6:2)! But there is an added dimension to the promise that is seldom stated: even a bad family experience *if properly processed* can turn out to be a grace-gift for the formation of a man or woman in Christ. To turn our hearts toward home is potentially to turn our hearts to God. *The Lost World of the Kalahari* describes the amazing sense of "home" that a Kalahari bushman had when he was even fifty miles from the sip-wells where he lived, with only twisted trails in between.

They were always centered. They knew without conscious effort, where their home was, as we had seen proved on many other more baffling occasions. Once indeed, more than a hundred and fifty miles from home, when asked where it lay they had instantly turned and pointed out the direction.[15]

In our so-called civilized world where we have lost our sense of home, we have lost our center. Perhaps the problem has been more accurately diagnosed by my friends in Kenya of the Kikuyu tribe who say that men working in the city with their wives living on the shamba (farm) have homes but not family. "We have a Kikuyu story," they tell me, "in which there is smoke coming through the roof of the thatched hut, but you find when you go in that the wood is too green to burn. There is smoke but no fire. There is a home but no family." But as we turn now to consider a case study in family spirituality, we are reassured that even in dysfunctional families, and families that hardly exist, there is potential not only to find God, but to be found by him.

5
Family
Feud

"In one sense one can portray the entire history of the people (of God) as the lengthened shadow of Jacob."—Kenneth Leech

There was a young man who cheated his brother, got everything he could out of his old man, and then ran away to live with relatives.[1] Then he fell in love and got married, only to discover he had wed the wrong woman. He became a successful businessman, but something was eating away inside him. It had to do with his alienated brother, his strange name, and his God.

The story of Jacob in Genesis 25–35 is a probing case study in domestic spirituality. It has been said that history is the lengthened shadow of a person. Therefore, as Kenneth Leech suggests, "In one sense one can portray the entire history of the people (of God) as the lengthened shadow of Jacob, a prolonged wrestling with God until the light dawns, *a process of perpetual interrogation and struggle*. It is this history of persons and communities in conflict which provides the content of revelation."[2]

It started with the way the boy was born, coming forth from the womb grabbing the heel of his twin brother, Esau. So they named him Jacob, which means "he who takes by the heel,"[3] as a wrestler pulls his opponent off balance by grabbing his heel. Cheater. Manipulator. Schemer. Imagine introducing yourself to a beautiful young woman when you have a name like that. Jacob, true to his name, manipulated his brother out of the birthright by which the oldest son would inherit two-thirds of the estate. Then he cheated him out of the blessing by which the promise of God's family would be passed on. He schemed to get the best of his father-in-law's flocks and herds by some dazzling genetic engineering. He tried to soften up his estranged brother with gifts. Jacob always had a plan, a scheme. Know anyone like that?

Jacob Meets Jacob

But God had a plan, too. And God's plan was first of all to bring Jacob to himself. God wanted to bless Jacob, but he could not do this until Jacob came to terms with himself. Jacob was always running away from his own name (and his own nature), and therefore running away from God's blessing. In *Death of a Salesman*, Mrs. Willie Loman provides this epitaph for her husband: "He didn't know who he was."[4] Jacob was also a man who did not know who he was, and he seemed determined not to find out. Many of us, like Jacob, live a false identity, one created around our jobs or adopted from media images, and spend decades in contriving such artful dodges. As R. D. Laing comments so insightfully, "It is as though we all preferred to die to preserve our shadows."[5] Tragically, the search for self in which the Western world now so passionately engages is a fruitless search since it is a search for what can only be given by another. Our identity is a gift of another's love.[6] And to set Jacob up for this gift, God had to plot a series of scenes to hold up mirrors to his life:

> *Scene 1.* God confronts Jacob with his own identity through his father's question: "Who are you, my son?" Jacob replies, "I am Esau your firstborn" (Gen. 27:19). He plays a role (complete with costume contrived by his mother, Rebekah) to help him trick his father, Isaac, into blessing him. When Esau finds his blessing has been stolen, he wants to kill his brother. Exit Jacob.

Scene 2. Enter Rachel, a beautiful young woman by the well in the land to which Jacob has fled. Jacob will not tell Rachel his name. He told Rachel that he was a relative of her father and a son of Rebekah (29:12). If my name was Cheat, I would not mention it either. Jacob does not admit his character to anyone. Yet.

Scene 3. Enter Laban, Rachel's father, whose behavior mirrors his own. While Jacob thinks he is marrying Laban's youngest daughter, Rachel, Laban slips in cross-eyed Leah behind the veil. Perhaps he had plied Jacob with wine to facilitate the deception. Just as Jacob dressed up in skins to imitate his brother, so Laban covers Leah to make Jacob think he has married Rachel. "What is this you have done to me?" (29:25) is equivalent to "Why have you been a Jacob to me?" Jacob meets another Jacob—a replay of the steal-the-blessing-from-your-brother act. Usually when we run away from home we end up pulling at the same old weeds in someone else's garden. This should give some pause to someone escaping into marriage.

Scene 4. Jacob has to face the music. God calls him to return to his homeland (31:13)—which means reuniting with Esau. Twenty years ago Esau wanted to kill him. Now Esau comes with four hundred men. Jacob prays! But he does some scheming too, as usual. Alone in the night, though, Jacob wrestles with God in the form of a man. Jacob is now a broken man. He has come to terms with himself. The God-man asks him the question he has been avoiding for twenty years: "What is your name?" (32:27). And Jacob, for the first time in the entire account, speaks his own name.

"'Jacob,' he answered" (32:27). It sounds too simple. But Jacob must be *himself* before God, not his brother, and not even the Jacob he would like to be. No more role playing, no vows and promises, no schemes and plans—just "Jacob." He has to let God deal with the real Jacob, the self whom God so patiently directed twenty years of conflicts to show him.

Frank Boreham notes that in his monumental *Journal*, John Wesley tells how before the light broke upon his soul at Aldersgate Street, he went to America with some vague idea of Christianizing the Indians.

> Almost as soon as he set foot upon the western continent, he made the acquaintance of Mr. Spangenberg, a German pastor. This devout and earnest man startled the newcomer by plying him with a succession of painfully penetrating and particularly uncomfortable questions. "Does the Spirit of God," he inquired, "bear witness with your spirit that you are a child of God?" Wesley was utterly bewildered and knew not how to reply. His confusion led the good German to ask his second question: "Do you know Jesus Christ?" Wesley hummed and haa-ed and at length answered feebly that he hoped that Christ had died to save him. Whereupon Mr. Spangenburg went one step further back. "Young man," he asked, "do you know *yourself?*" Wesley replied that he did, but he confesses that his answer lacked sincerity and conviction.[7]

> Like the prodigal in Jesus' tale, Jacob can only come to the Father if he comes to himself. And like that New Testament prodigal Jacob can only come to himself because he has a Father to whom he can return. So the heel-grabber is no longer called Jacob but Israel. No longer "cheater," but "he who strives with God"—a new name and a new person, limping and broken but knowing now that he belongs to God. Even the bruise became transfigured as a daily reminder that Jacob's weakness took him to the God who made his strength perfect in weakness. The German philosopher Adolf Alexander Schroeders expressed this provocatively in these words: "My burden carries me."[8]

Jacob Meets His Family

God's plan, secondly, was to bring Jacob to terms with his family. If I were God and wanted to rescue the human race and reveal my own character, I would never think of doing it through a family. Even if I did, I am sure I would not choose this one, the family of Abraham, Isaac, and Jacob. It was a mess.

1. There was favoritism in it. "Isaac, who had a taste for wild game, loved Esau, but Rebekah loved Jacob" (Gen. 25:28). This resulted in envy, hostility, and twenty years of separation between the brothers. Esau never felt accepted and tried pathetically to please his parents by his choice of wives (28:8-9)—some reason to get married! Jacob lapped up his mother's favoritism and learned to live that way, so he too had a favorite wife, Rachel (29:30), with the resultant envy, jealousy, and alienation. Then Jacob had a favorite child, Joseph, who was almost murdered by his brothers. The sins of the fathers were visited upon the children unto the third and fourth generations (Exod. 20:5).

2. The traditional family roles were reversed. Isaac was a weak leader; Rebekah, a manipulating, unsubmissive wife. Perhaps Isaac had married for the wrong reasons. He was over forty, and his mother had just died. (You can light a candle most easily just after it has been extinguished.) "Isaac brought her into the tent of his mother Sarah, and he married Rebekah. So she became his wife, and he loved her; and Isaac was comforted after his mother's death" (Gen. 24:67). You can read between the lines. In spite of the prophecy that the elder son would serve the younger (25:23), Isaac went ahead and blessed his favorite. Rebekah lied and schemed against her husband to get him to bless her choice, Jacob (27:1-40). She, like her son, would not trust God to do it his way, or wait for God to bring to fruition his own intention declared in the prenatal prophecy (25:23).

3. There was alienation in that family—between parents, between sons, between wives, between children, between children and in-laws. Jacob left home with unresolved tensions with his parents and his brother. He suffered twenty years of separation from his family and therefore twenty years apart from God. No one can be right with God and wrong with his brother and sister. As Kenneth Leech says,

Jewish experience of God, from Abraham to the present, has been the experience of people in solidarity with each other, responsible for each other. "Where is your brother?" (Gen. 4:9, RSV) has remained across the centuries, a fundamental test of discipleship. "Unless your . . . brother comes down with you, you shall see my face no more" (Gen. 44:23) might be seen as God's own words to his people. For it is in community that God makes his presence known.[9]

4. But the most important factor is the reason for this family's story in the Bible. *God was in that family.* But, given the complexity of this family, where was God?

God had given his promise of blessing to this family, and he would not revoke it (Gen. 17:4ff). For all the promises of God find their "Yes" in Christ (2 Cor. 1:20).

God was simply *with* them, even though they sometimes did not know it. The runaway Jacob was given a vision of God's presence (Gen. 28:10-22). The day after he cheated his brother, God said to him, "I am with you" (28:15). God graciously gave him the gift of faithful human love. "So Jacob served seven years to get Rachel, but they seemed like only a few days to him because of his love for her" (29:20). Most people will not wait even a few months to possess the object of their love. When Jacob prospered on his father-in-law's ranch, he had to admit it was because of his God: "If the God of my father . . . had not been with me . . ." (31:42). And then through that dramatic night encounter with the angel, God broke him and healed him. "I saw God face to face, and yet my life was spared," he said (32:30). Even in the far country God never left him.

Michael Novak once said that "the point of marriage and family is to make us realistic."[10] God took the members of this family through difficult lessons in reality to bring them to maturity and faith. Isaac was a worldly, sensuous man who loved to eat his hunter-son Esau's game. He lived to see Esau choose pagan wives that "were a source of grief to Isaac and Rebekah" (Gen. 26:35).

Rebekah, a scheming, manipulative wife with a favorite son, lost him from the family circle. Esau had contempt for his birthright and lost it and the blessing of the firstborn son, though he later sought it with tears (Heb. 12:17). Jacob, the heel-grabber, stole his brother's birthright and blessing. God let him have his way. But he had to run for his life, chased by his father-in-law (Gen. 31:23). His only daughter was raped (Gen. 34). His beloved and favorite wife died in childbirth (35:17-19). His favorite son, Joseph, was kidnapped and sold into slavery. God lets us have what we say we want, but we inevitably become realistic through it all.

There is, however, a surprise. One of the infallible marks of God's personhood and presence is the irruption of the unexpected. Barren Rachel was miraculously given a child. Unloved and rejected Leah was chosen to continue the line of God's promise, and after Rachel died, Leah seems to have been loved. She, and not Rachel, was buried beside Jacob (Gen. 49:29-31).

Jacob? God graciously brought him to himself, a broken but saved man. He was reconciled to his brother and saw in him the face of God (Gen. 33:10). God had brought each of them to the point of knowing that their needs could not be met by anyone but God himself. Each parent looked to a favorite child for satisfaction and was disappointed. Isaac looked to Esau, who made life bitter for him, and Rebekah looked to Jacob, who had to run for his life. Jacob got married but was still Jacob. Marriage did not solve his problems. His burdens carried him to the Lord. It was when "Jacob was left alone" that he found God. No other idols. Remember the hard saying of Jesus that one must hate father, mother, wife, and children to be his follower (Luke 14:26)? We must let Christ meet our needs. And he introduces us to a bigger, better family (Luke 18:29-30).

Jacob Meets the Family God

Finally, God's plan was to bring Jacob to terms with God himself, and to do this through his family experience. There is maximum inspiration in the phrase "the God of Abraham, Isaac, and Jacob." In that is the seed of the gospel of Jesus, who came not to call the righteous, but sinners, to repentance. God loves heel-grabbers and saves them. He is a God of grace. He works through the sensuality of Isaac, the scheming of Rebekah, the deception of Jacob. He is also a God who calls—and his call is a promise. "Yet I have loved Jacob, but Esau I have hated" (Mal. 1:2) hardly sounds like grace from the mouth of God. But, as Spurgeon once said, it is not surprising that God hated Esau; what is truly amazing is that God loved Jacob. As James Stewart once said, "It was Jephthah, not Jehovah, who said, 'Why are you come to me now when you are in distress?'" (Judg. 11:7, NKJV).

> God will not stop to inquire into the motives when a nation in peril of its existence or a whole recalcitrant generation returns to Him at last, any more than He inquires into the motives of one lost soul limping home from the far country. Even if the motive is mainly self-preservation— "How many . . . have bread enough and to spare, and I perish with hunger!" (Luke 15:17, NKJV)[11]

Jacob and Esau embody the mystery of God's gracious call. God does not reject some in order to save others. In fact, he calls some to save everyone else who will hear the call. His call is not judgment, but sheer mercy. In his grace he allows us to resist his mercy, as Esau apparently did. Esau seemed like the winner at the starting line—an all-around man. We would have placed our bets on him. Like the older brother in the parable of the Prodigal Son, he stayed at home and did what his father wanted. If the parable of the two prodigals in the New Testament (Luke 15:11-32) speaks to good people by showing us an elder brother who lived a good life but did not understand the father's heart (15:28-32)—the story of Jacob and Esau in the Old Testament speaks to good believers whose hearts have not yet broken with gratitude. Esau was satisfied with the life he created for himself. He did not care for the promise of God. Jacob, on the other hand, cared so much for the promise that he would cheat to get it. He always wanted more. And he got it. But being transformed by grace is costly. Here is what Jacob had to undergo to come to terms with God.

First, he had to discover that he could not manipulate God. He thought he had God well-managed. So he was too confident to be blessed. He could scheme his way through every situation to keep God well-contained. He could make it through life on his own, he thought. But he had to learn that he could not trust himself or his own work. At Bethel, God graciously met him as a runaway cheat. But Jacob's response was a conditional vow, a contractual bargain: "If God will be with me . . . then the LORD will be my God" (Gen. 28:20-21). Later, he would be ready to relinquish his own will. Jacob had to face his brother in the end, but he contrived to win his favor with wave after wave of gifts (32:13-15), like those clever Christmas gifts that achieve maximum psychological impact by inviting you to open box within box. Later, he would discover the grace of God in the face of the person whom he most feared (33:10).

Jacob had to want God and his blessing more than anything. Jacob came to the place of demanding the blessing of

God. "I will not let you go, unless you bless me," he said to the angel. It was the first time he did not scheme. He was a beggar before God. No, it is more accurate to say he fought with God to get God. Jesus said that people enter the kingdom by violence (Luke 16:16, RSV), because the kingdom is for the desperate, not the mildly interested. Jacob would not let the night pass without God's blessing. Therefore he was given a new name, Israel, for he had "struggled with God and with men and *overcame*" (Gen. 32:28, italics mine).

Finally, Jacob had to clear his life of all that hindered worship of God. Twenty years after he had left home, the Hound of Heaven caught up with him. It was another ten years before Jacob kept his vow to return to Bethel and build an altar. At last he put away foreign gods and purified himself and family to live a life of worship.

Jacob finished well. We might have chosen Esau, but God chose Jacob; and Jacob finished with God, the God of Abraham, Isaac, and Jacob, the God and Father of our Lord Jesus Christ, the God who loves heel-grabbers.

The story of Jacob is full of grace-notes for people spending a day with their families. God is at work in our lives even before we are born. God comes to us even when we are running away from our families. God gives us more than we deserve in our spouses, our children, and our parents. God gives us grace to accept what we cannot change in our family backgrounds. All of us, like Jacob, inherit family baggage. All of us must choose whether we will reflect the worst of our family background, or turn the liabilities of our families into assets. God has borne the garbage of our family past and present, as we now know through the cross of Jesus (1 Pet. 2:24).

Our lives, like Jacob's, can end with family blessing (Gen. 49). The story of Jacob ends with a revealing incident. His son Joseph brought his two children, Manasseh, the oldest, and Ephraim, the youngest, to be blessed by the patriarch before he died. But Jacob put his right hand, normally reserved for the firstborn, and crossed his arms, placing his right hand on the head of the youngest so the younger would be first (48:13-15). Joseph complained, "No, my father, this one is the firstborn; put your right hand on his head." Jacob refused and said, "I know, my son, I know" (48:18-19). What Jacob knew was that what makes a family into a domestic church is not natural perfection or human accomplishment but the undeserved grace of God.

Home is not simply the place where, when you have to go there they have to take you in. The old farmer's wife said it correctly and deeply, "I should have called it something you somehow haven't to deserve."

6
Raising Godly Parents

"In our society, of course, there is no need to become an adult. One may remain—one is exhorted daily to remain—a child forever. . . . To have children is plainly to cease being a child oneself."—Michael Novak

Most books and articles on Christian education in the home are preoccupied with raising godly children. Yet the Bible emphasizes raising godly parents. Children are God's gifts to immature adults to help them grow up. Now we must explore how children are God's gifts to help parents go deep with God. It turns out that raising parents is child's work. But to explore this paradox we must first deal with a ubiquitous misunderstanding.

Domestic Holiness
Family life domesticates the spirituality of parents. It takes spirituality out of the realm of the religious and places it irrevocably in the realm of the ordinary. Unfortunately family spirituality has often been understood as how to make the children "mind" and how to conduct family devotions. In this we have not moved much beyond the family spirituality of the sixteenth century. Thomas Bacon in his "Catechism set forth dialogue-wise between the father and the son" described his duty as ruler over his six-year-old son with these words: "For every householder's house ought to be a

school of godliness, for as much as every householder ought to be a bishop in his own house, and so oversee his family that nothing reign in it but virtues, godliness and honesty."[1] Because this attitude was being promoted, a spate of books of family prayers poured out of the Puritan presses in England. Much of this amounted to moving the monastic spirituality out of the cloister and into the home without viewing the relationship itself as the context of spiritual formation.

The second Vatican council's emphasis on the family as a "domestic sanctuary" did little to correct this misunderstanding. The council stated that the family is "the first and vital cell of society" and the "domestic sanctuary of the Church"[2] through mutual affection, common prayer, and liturgical worship. Fortunately some contemporary Catholic reflection on this goes much farther in exploring the idea that *the family itself*, as a communal image of the Holy Trinity, is a sacrament in at least three ways: First, each member of the family is designed by God to be a vessel of grace to other members as they help each other make life more endurable, hopeful, and glorious. Second, the family has apostolic potential since it provides a haven in a heartless world and expresses the importance of the *personal* in an increasingly private and impersonal culture. And finally, the family in Christ is sacramental because family life calls us to live beyond ourselves.[3] As Frederick Parella says, "Achieving one's life by giving it up is hardly a popular idea in an age of individualism, self-reliance, and self-fulfilment,"[4] but it is exactly what family life evokes.

This approach is deliciously close to the emphasis Luther brought to the subject of domestic holiness. Luther upheld the domestic vocation against both the pagan and monastic devaluation of it by emphasizing that what makes a family Christian is not the religious activity, but faith.

Now you tell me, when a father goes ahead and washes diapers or performs some other mean task for his child, and someone ridicules him as an effeminate fool—though that father is acting in the spirit just described and in Christian faith—my dear fellow you tell me, which of the two is most keenly ridiculing the other? God with all his angels and creatures is smiling—not because that father is washing diapers, but because he is doing so in Christian faith.[5]

Parental Submission

The Christian education of would-be parents begins with the experience of "leaving father and mother" in order to form a covenant. A marriage is not Christian because it is contrived by two Christians who marry in a church, or because it is certified by a clergyperson, but because it is crafted according to God's design: "For this reason a man will leave his father and mother and be united to his wife, and they will become one flesh" (Gen. 2:24).[6] In every culture of the world the woman is expected to leave father and mother in order to cleave to her husband. But the Bible requires even the man to change his first allegiance from parents to spouse. In rural Africa it is customary for the wife to move into the shamba (farm) of the husband's parents. And that same practice was in effect in my mother's generation, when men brought their wives into their parents' home in the little fishing village in Newfoundland where my mother was born. So when Gail and I get into marriage discussions in Africa we often ask a probing question: Should married men obey their parents? "Of course," is the standard reply. We are always careful in the vigorous discussion that follows to show how difficult it is for North American couples to leave their parents *emotionally* even though they easily leave home physically. And we have little to say about the success rate of the American model! What we are trying to do is to let God speak his redemptive word into both cultures.

One of the things we often point out in these discussions is that *obey* (Eph. 6:1) and *honor* (Exod. 20:12) are not the same thing. Obviously, obeying parents—as commanded in Ephesians—is a word to immature children under the direct supervision and control of their parents. Honoring father and mother—as required in the fifth commandment—is a lifelong call that includes obedience during the years of minority, but positively requires changing the obedience pattern when one "leaves father and mother" in order to "unite" with one's spouse (Gen. 2:24). Married people must usually stop submitting to their parents, except in the sense of voluntarily serving them with perpetual honor.

Wise parents make this easy for couples who marry, but in reality this is seldom easy anywhere in the world. The refusal to move from honoring parents by obedience to honoring without obedience frustrates the formation of the marriage covenant and is the source of much pain in marriage. Few persons can please their parents and their spouses at the same time in lifestyle, parenting, vocational choices, and religious choice. Such misdirected honoring appears to be obedience, but in reality it is disobedience to God's revealed marital order. And no amount of religious activity or spiritual disciplines can compensate for this intergenerational sin.

However, once the husband-wife covenant is firmly established, family spirituality continues to require honoring parents, even through the difficulties most couples experience with their parents and in-laws. Most parents are not emotionally prepared to "let go" of their children in order to relate to them as adult to adult. This is a spiritual issue and an invitation to go deeper with God as parents. But patience on the part of the newly married "children" is one concrete form of giving worth to their parents during what must inevitably be a process. God is not finished making either the parents of the children or the children of the parents. At every age children help parents grow up.

Honoring means never renouncing them as parents and fulfilling the appropriate roles of care and respect for those persons, who will always be family for us. We do for parents what we can, not merely what we must, especially when they grow older and need greater care. This is especially relevant for parents-in-law, who are the butt of so many cruel jokes. When a mother-in-law rearranges the dishes in the cupboards of a young wife's kitchen to suit the mother-in-law's taste, there must be no question where the husband's loyalty is directed. At the same time there is a mother-in-law to be honored. If this does not call forth personal and spiritual maturity then nothing can!

But now we must turn to the parenting role itself. The passage in Ephesians 6:1-4 is often used to expound the duty of training of children in the faith: "Fathers . . . bring them up in the training and instruction of the Lord" (6:4). But the prior injunction—"Do not exasperate your children"— makes a greater demand on the parents than on their children. Instead of breaking the will of strong-willed children, Paul requires breaking the parent's angry will. Parents are not to frustrate and antagonize their children with unreasonable demands or unrestrained anger. Paul's interest is not primarily in how to deliver Christian education to children through Bible reading and family devotions, good as these are. His interest is not in technique but in *relationships*, not so much in the content imparted as the context implied. Therefore he speaks of the "nurture and admonition of the Lord."

Training in the Greek original *(paideia)* suggests the nurturing, developing, building, and washing ministry Jesus has with his disciples.[7] *Instruction* or *admonition* means loving correction, affirming confrontation. Again, parents experience this ministry from Jesus *with* their children, not merely transmitting it *to* their children. The context for all of this instruction is Ephesians 5:21: "Submit to one another out of reverence for Christ." Paul gives three examples of mutual submission in 5:22–6:9: husband and wife, employer and employee, and parents and children. Each of these three is counter-cultural. Paul calls not only children to submit to their parents, but parents to their children, husbands to wives, employers to employees.

The submission of parents to the needs of the child is especially important in three crucial areas: providing affirmation, limits, and a future with promise. Affirmation meets a deep need in a child to feel loved and unconditionally accepted. It is unfair to demand good behaviour without first making a child certain that he or she is loved. If the child cannot please his parents, when a child's frustration is not understood, when a child feels that good is never good enough, when a child feels that behavior is more important than belonging, then he or she is provoked to anger. The anger can be expressed in temper, bad behavior, and dangerous sexual adventures, or suppressed until it surfaces later in life. Establishing limits and correcting means that the child must know that he or she is not omnipotent. *Paideia* is more concerned with guidance than punishment, but correction is sometimes needed. Punishment by itself has limited value, as the following story suggests.

James Dobson tells the story of a father who stopped his car, took his three kids out, spanked them all, put them back in the car, and solemnly warned them that they were not allowed to say anything for thirty minutes. They drove along the highway and thirty minutes later the little girl said, "Mommy, may I speak now?" "Yes, I guess so." "Well, back there where Daddy spanked me, I lost one shoe!" There is much more to the *instruction* and *admonition* of the Lord than this.

The third fundamental need of every child, to have a future with promise, is crucial for people being raised in a generation that has lost any sense of a worthwhile end to which the travail of history might lead. Christians breathe hope in the bleakest of moments. Affirmation, limits, and hope: providing each of these three calls forth a deeper spirituality in the parents.

Every child needs to be loved unconditionally, but has the parent experienced the unconditional love of Jesus? The parent is "being raised" in the context of the Lord's instruction alongside the child. Every child needs to be prized not for what he or she does, but simply for who he or she is. Has the parent discovered on the experiential level that we have a God who counts relationship more important than behavior? Every child needs to be freed from the tyranny of perfectionism. Has the parent learned that God is looking not for the perfect parent but for one who parents with faith, hope, and love? Every child needs to be shown a future with hope, no matter how bleak society may appear. Does the parent have such a hope? Every child's need, question, and longing is a silent prayer that the parents will find God to be their all-in-all. In Ephesians 6:1-4, Paul invites parents to draw their children into the Lord's parenting by making sure that they as parents are being parented by the Lord. For if the parents live for their children they will destroy not only their children but themselves.

Parenting as Hospitality

One helpful way of expressing the mystery of the parent-child relationship "in the Lord" (Eph. 6:1), is to speak of parenting as giving hospitality. In this ambivalent age of parenting when parents seem to oscillate between *smothering* and *dumping* their children, it is crucial for parents to explore their role as hosts and stewards, rather than ultimate owners. The child belongs to God. And therefore parent and child are "in the Lord" whether all the family members are Christians or not. Therefore, the parent has no right to keep or control him or her. Each child will have his or her own style, interests, and potentials. Children keep surprising their parents unless they are continuously emotionally squashed or forcefully molded into the parents' image.

Henri Nouwen speaks of "the little stranger at home," and of children as "our most important guests" and people "who carry a promise with them, a hidden treasure that has to be led into the open through education."[8] His words are worth pondering deeply:

> What parents can offer is a home, a place that is receptive but also has safe boundaries within which their children can develop and discover what is helpful and what is harmful. . . . The awareness that children are guests can be a liberating awareness because many parents suffer from deep guilt feelings toward their children, thinking they are responsible for everything their sons and daughters do.[9]

In contrast to Nouwen's approach, many parents want their own way and demand the production of immediate Christians in their family. Parents with God's interests want their children to come into their teens hungry for God and fascinated with Jesus, not stuffed with unapplied Christian information. If, in due course, their children become true believers, it will not be the result of their superlative parenting. If the children do not profess faith, it does not necessarily mean the parents did a poor job. People are saved by grace, not by works, not even the parents' works. But God is ultimately interested not in how the race starts but in how it ends. The parable of the two prodigals (Luke 15:11-32) is an eloquent invitation to parents to leave the outcome to God and to keep their hearts open to their children no matter what they do with their faith. But if children do embrace Jesus as their Lord, then the children become priests to the parents. Otherwise the priesthood of all believers would be only for grown-ups.

Luther once said that God has given two institutions for our sanctification: the church and the home. Of the two, the home is an everyday opportunity to find and be found by God. Parenting is like one giant, continuous, worldwide evangelistic crusade to bring us back to God. How ludicrous it is to talk of professional parenting. To assign the parenting service to a paid professional robs the real parents of the ministry their children can have to them. God has ordained that the family will be the primary arena for spiritual formation. The church might make Sunday school the center of Christian nurture, but the home will always win out, for good or ill. Dennis Guernsey, a family sociologist, says that this means that the primary task of the church is to parent parents.[10] A day with the family is a day of being constantly invited to let God be God. Each moment of the day we are invited to let the Holy Spirit get into us enough to *serve* the people closest to us in life.

I had the privilege of preaching in Montreal at the ordination of Joseph Hovsepian. He pastors a multiethnic congregation but supports himself by running an electronics store in Montreal. He is the first lay pastor to be ordained or commissioned within his denomination within the last sixty-five years, and there was no way I was going to miss the occasion.

But during the ordination service his two teenaged daughters interrupted the published program with an unscheduled duet. Then the oldest took the microphone unannounced and said, "I want you to know what it is like in our home. Home isn't perfect. We have our good and our bad moments as a family. But I can assure you that my father is the same person at home as he is in the pulpit. And we respect and love him." God is at home in this man's home.

Parenting is not *for* anything. It is not a contract with God in which one gives countless hours in order to turn out good children that rise up and call us blessed. It is a covenant experience of belonging in which God meets us and forms us in the nitty-gritty of family life. The big question in the end is not how the kids turn out, but how the parents turn out!

PART THREE

A DAY WITH THE
OTHER
SEX

7

Contemplative Sexuality

"God seemingly had to take all sorts of risks in order that we would not miss the one thing necessary: we had to be called and even driven out of ourselves by an almost insatiable appetite so that we would never presume we were self-sufficient."—Richard Rohr

In the old days people would turn to a chapter on sex first! In those days it was said there are two kinds of people in the world: those who are interested in sex, and liars! But a chapter on *contemplative* sexuality today hardly seems to fit the aspirations of our society, which pretends to be the most sexually sophisticated generation on earth. In reality it may be one of the most impoverished because of its preoccupation with technique. To understand ourselves sexually the question that must be addressed is not "how to" but "how come?" If we attend to this latter question, a day with the opposite sex (or a portion of every day) can become an invitation to Godwardness. But to do so is countercultural.

On the one hand we are experiencing a tragic drift in Western society toward androgyny; people demand unisex everything: haircuts, clothes, employment opportunities, marriage roles, and ministry in the church. On the other hand, sexuality has been reduced to genital activity, and the fig leaf has been ripped off. In reality, merged and explicit sex is reduced sex, sexuality with the mystery removed. Biblical Christians must recover a contemplative approach to the mystery of male and female. Such contemplation will take us beyond the current fad of speaking of the sacredness of sex—which may often amount to the deification of eroticism—in order to explore the transcendent meaning of having been created male and female in God's image. By thus pursuing the implicit rather than the explicit meaning of being male and female we will find that the mystery of sexuality is a reason for faith and a way to turn to God himself. In this chapter we will explore three contemplative approaches to the sexual mystery. Later we will consider three areas of application: ministry, authentic singleness, and marriage.

Recovering the Mystery of Male and Female

Fundamental to the recovery of the mystery is the archetypal passage in Genesis 1:27: "In the image of God he created him; male and female he created them." Humankind is an icon of God, a poetic masterpiece, an artistic expression of God's own personhood. God literally thought us up as a work of art and spoke us into existence. We were in the mind's eye of God as graphic art, and then we were crafted. God composed us inwardly as a beautiful melody even before the tune could be put down, and then God breathed into us a portion of his own being. As God's image we *are* God's imagination. Even though we are a scarred and twisted representation because of sin, we are both a symbol and a metaphor of the Creator: symbol in the sense of a visual representation of a transcendent truth, and metaphor in the sense of a word picture that evokes a deep but otherwise allusive truth. This takes us beyond the biology, psychology, and sociology of sex to explore its spirituality.

But humankind is a social metaphor. So God created two sexes, in order that the longing to be together of the two sexes would be evocative of authentic life in God. The male by himself is incapable of being the full image of God. So is the female. It takes both sexes in relationship to each other to express God in a human metaphor. Neither the fall into sin nor the substantial redemption accomplished by Christ alters the essential truth that male and female are *together* the image of God. Therefore God-likeness is a social reality. True spirituality is interpersonal, relational. Relationships are pathways to God.

So the purpose of human sexuality is not merely for procreation,[1] or for the mutual blessing of covenant partners, though both are good in themselves. Sexuality was designed to be first and finally contemplative so that we would seek God himself. Whether we marry and procreate, or remain as singles celebrating sexual diversity in a co-sexual community, sexuality is designed to turn us toward God, to make us prayerful, and to evoke our faith. Unfortunately much contemporary biblical scholarship seems determined either to reduce the mystery to clearly defined roles and hierarchies that require no faith, or to dissolve the mystery into egalitarian togetherness with no difference except for the genitals. It is my conviction that the complexity—even the ambiguity—of Scripture on this subject deepens rather than reduces the mystery.

The Ambiguity of Scripture

Competent biblical scholars line up on both sides of the women's ministry debate. Some defend what they call parity of the sexes at home and in the church; others defend distinctive roles and governmental differences between the sexes.[2] Both groups claim the authority of Scripture. It is a frustrating situation. The debate seems to have hit an impasse, with many people "solving" the problem by finding churches where everyone already agrees with their position. To me this seemed less than ideal. And yet what were the alternatives? I did not want merely to add my voice to the polemical chorus. And then I had a thought: What if the ambiguity at the root of the differences is not accidental but inspired? What if God's Word intentionally puts us in a bind, a bind that only faith can resolve.

On the one hand, the Bible teaches radical sexual equality in creation and in Christ as illustrated by the following observations:

- Both sexes are created in the image of God (Gen. 1:26-28).
- Full side-by-side complementarity of the sexes is God's intended plan (Gen. 2:18-25).
- In Christ, the curse experienced by male and female is substantially reversed. Instead of the politics of rule and revolt in the home (Gen. 3:16),[3] there is the grace of mutual submission (Eph. 5:21-33).
- Males and females enjoy full equality in Christ (Gal. 3:28).
- Men and women are joint heirs of the spiritual gifts (1 Cor. 12:1-31) and coleaders (Acts 2:17-18) of God's people under the new covenant.[4]
- Each marriage partner is given authority over the other's body, a revolutionary principle in the first century (1 Cor. 7:5).

So the advocates of female equality and interchangeable ministries seem to have the Bible on their side. But so do those who insist that sexual differences are entrenched in Creation and exalted by Christ. Here is another sampling of observations:

- The physical constitution of each sex suggests that there are profound differences in both psychology and spirituality, differences that are incarnated in the norms and traditions of every culture and have profound implications for our spiritualities (Gen. 2:18-25).[5]

- Though Paul modifies his own argument (1 Cor. 11:11), he finds in the creation of woman *from* man (1 Cor. 11:8), *for* man (11:9), and *after* man (1 Tim. 2:13) an argument for some kind of male priority, not merely in the culture of his day but entrenched in Creation.
- Three corrective passages in Scripture insist that sexual distinctions must be made in ministry (1 Cor. 11:3-16; 14:34-35; 1 Tim. 2:11-15).[6]
- The husband is head of the wife as Christ is head of the church (Eph. 5:23).[7]
- The Bible is rich in feminine imagery of God (e.g. Pss. 22:9; 123:2), but there is not a single case in the Bible where we are exhorted or encouraged to call God "Mother."[8] To speak of God as Father is fundamental to biblical faith.

Thus Scripture presents us with two seemingly irreconcilable truths. So how can we resolve the bind in which this leaves us? Contemplation provides the clue. If humankind—male and female—is a social metaphor of God himself (Gen. 1:27), then we must relate the mystery of sexuality to the mystery of God himself.

The Ultimate Mystery

Christians of evangelical persuasion—of which I am one—typically approach issues rationally and systematically. Arguments for and against the ordination of women have been made in this mode. But while proponents believe they have God's view of the matter, their viewpoint brings with it certain unconfessed presuppositions—namely, that the fundamental truths of Scripture *can* be systematized, which will then eliminate all paradoxes and yield unequivocal answers.

I am proposing an alternative method—the contemplative approach. This approach views the ambiguity of Scripture as a pointer to God, an indicator of truths so great that they can only be seen from God-height. A contemplative view takes seriously the fact that the Bible is more often historical than abstract, more often narrative and metaphorical than systematic. A contemplative approach welcomes the mystery of male and female as an occasion of worship more than debate.

A mystery takes us beyond normal human categories of thought to explore incomprehensible fact, transcendent truth, and realities that will be appreciated more through worship than through simple cognition. Scripture offers three such mysteries: the mystery of sexuality, the mystery of Christ and the church (Eph. 5:32), and the mystery of Jew and Gentile in a new humanity (Eph. 3:6; 2:11-22). All three mysteries point us toward the transcendent unity within God himself (Eph. 4:4-6), a unity that is a social complex. To focus on the mystery of sexuality requires *under*standing— rather than *over*-standing—God. In humility we stand under and worship Father, Son, and Holy Spirit, in whose image we are made male and female. Contemplative sexuality must be thoroughly Trinitarian not only in theology but in worship.

The theological parallel for androgyny (the merging of the sexes, or the desexualization of humanity) is Islamic monotheism or Unitarianism. The impoverished unity in each case results in abstraction rather than personhood. A Muslim does not call God "Abba." The central creed of Islam, that there is but one God, is surprisingly Christianity's most profound doctrine. Father, Son, and Holy Spirit are diverse but gloriously one. Social Trinitarianism proclaims a unity in God deeper than the abstract unity of Islam. Perhaps the ultimate irony in the history of religions is that, far from proclaiming tritheism, the Christian church humbly confesses the deepest truth of the Muslim creed: One God. And we do this by insisting that we have come to know God as Father, Son, and Holy Spirit. J. I. Packer says, "God is not only *he* but also *they*—Father, Son and Spirit, coequal and coeternal in power and glory though functioning in a set pattern whereby the Son obeys the Father and the Spirit subserves both."[9] That is the mystery of the Holy Trinity and the focus of contemplative sexuality.

The Orthodox church has best understood the awesome beauty of the Trinity. While the Western Church, starting with Augustine, began with the philosophical notion of the unity of the Godhead and then attempted to explain the differences of the persons, the Eastern Church started with the apostolic witness, and the church's experience of three divine persons, and then explored, as an act of worship, the marvelous unity within the Godhead. Within Orthodox spirituality "the divine Trinity is the fundamental mystery of the Christian faith."[10] In other words, God is more one because he is three.[11]

If humankind is an artistic expression of God's personhood we will be more one because we are two. And we discover that unity not primarily through the physical embrace, but by experiencing God. According to Orthodox spirituality, Christian experience is nothing more or less than being included in the unity of the Trinity, participating in the mutual love, order, and interdependence of the three persons of the Holy Trinity. Fellowship is not camaraderie or likemindedness. It is the mystery of God replicated, albeit imperfectly, in the mystery of the church, the mystery of marriage, and the mystery of sexuality. The life of the Trinity then becomes the model for relationships with the family of God and the human family generally.

When Christ prayed that "they may be one as we are" (John 17:11, 25-26), he was not merely praying that individual believers would be united with God, but that believers would participate in the social unity of the Trinity while they experience loving communion with one another. Speaking to this, James Houston says, "To know the Triune God is to act like Him, in self-giving, in interdependence, and in boundless love."[12] We should not cheapen this mystery either by unisexing the church or by compartmentalizing the sexes in the church: women ministering to women and men to both men and women. This is the one community on earth that claims to bear the image of the triune God.

An axiom of the spiritual life is that we become like the God we worship. Idol-worshippers become fixed and inexpressive like their gods (Ps. 115:8). Trinity-worshippers become celebrators of community and cohumanity. If humankind is created in the image of God, and if both the marriage couple and the church are a mystery of Christ, then we discover our true sexuality through a worshipful imitation of our triune God in the living out of our lives.

The full emancipation of the sexes (both male and female) in the last analysis calls for a spiritual, more than a psychosocial or political, solution. Just as sexual perversions are not mainly matters of biology or psychology, but reflect misdirected contemplation (Rom. 1:18-32), sexual health is primarily an issue of faith. We become like the God we worship. Prayer is more important than politics in bringing peace to the battle of the sexes.

Followers of Jesus have a unique contribution in healing the confusion of the sexes today. We do this by welcoming liberation of women and men, and simultaneously by refusing to undermine sexual distinctiveness. We proudly proclaim that women's liberation really started with Mary, who was accorded the highest honor given any human being, that of being the Christ-bearer. We gladly exonerate the much-maligned apostle Paul, who insisted that women were not second class-citizens.

At the same time, the church has a special contribution in prizing the difference. We should resist the unisexing of everything, including, if not especially, the unisexing of marriage partners and the unisexing of church ministers. Positively put, we should equip the saints to welcome the mystery of male and female as a path to God. That is what a contemplative approach to sexuality offers. We will explore this first in relation to ministry, then to marriage, and finally to singleness.

8
Full Partnership in Ministry

An imaginary interview with C. S. Lewis on the subject of men and women might take this shape:

RPS: Dr. Lewis, I understand that you are not really convinced about the equality of the sexes.

CSL: I have the highest regard for the opposite sex. But there is no equality anywhere. In the great deep dance of heaven there is no equality. We are not like stones laid side by side, or one on top of the other, but stones ordered in an archway with each of us interlocking with Him, the center. We are all equally at the center, and none are there by being equals.[1]

RPS: But whether you use the word *equality* or not, both men and women are needed in church leadership equally, since both men and women are made in the image of God.

CSL: Only a man in a masculine uniform can represent God to the church, since the church is essentially feminine to God.[2]

RPS: Dr. Lewis, your argument is curiously reversible. If only men in masculine uniforms can be in church leadership because church leaders represent God to the church, then is it not true that only women in feminine uniforms should be in church leadership when those leaders offer sacrifices of praise and worship? If the church is the bride and Christ is the groom, then the ministers and those appointed to act on behalf of the church must all be women! Is it not more faithful to biblical theology and more fruitful for biblical doxology, for men and women *to serve together* in full ministry and leadership partnership and so more fully reflect God's glory by being his social image?[3]

I am sure that C. S. Lewis would explain that he is not depreciating women, not against female leadership or women in ministry, but repulsed by the modern addiction to the idea of equality. He would probably want to point out that while the Bible exalts sexual differences, it sees no differences in the rights and privileges of men and women when they are in Christ. But that leaves us with a dilemma that must be resolved if peace is to come to the battle of the sexes in the church and home. How can these sexual differences be expressed in marriage and ministry so that *both* equality and differences are honored?

The pastor who officiated at Gail's and my wedding once said, "There are three kinds of people: men, women, and ministers." This quip was greeted years ago with gales of laughter. Today people might snicker or get upset. But Tom Allen was unintentionally prophetic when he repeated what he considered a popular misconception. Now it has become a deep problem. *Ministry has become neutered.*

God's design is male and female in full and equal partnership. But in some cases, in the modern world, our practice of full partnership lags behind the actual practice of churches in the first century. And the practice in the primitive churches often lagged behind the teaching of the inspired apostles, as it did, for example, on the issue of slavery.

Ministry Partnership in the New Testament

In New Testament times women found so much freedom in Christ that the guidelines many people take to be rules were *corrections* to the abuse of a wonderful freedom, a freedom no longer granted in many quarters. We must ask whether women today are as liberated as they were under the apostolic leadership of the much-maligned apostle Paul. Do we need today the corrective word of the apostle that women should "shut up," "remain silent" (1 Cor. 14:34), "learn in quietness" (1 Tim. 2:11), "not to teach" (even women and children) (1 Tim. 2:12), and certainly not to domineer men (for that is the most likely meaning of the Greek word for "authority" in 1 Tim. 2:12)? Are women going so far in their new freedom in Christ that they are taking off their wedding rings as they enter the church and saying, in effect, "I don't have to relate to my husband as a wife or my father as a daughter now that I am in Christ" (for that is what the veiling issue means today, 1 Cor. 11:3-16)? Are women in the church today inflicting their anger on their former male suppressors? Does the apostle's word need to rebuke women who claim to have a superior spirituality, "Did the word of God originate with you?" (1 Cor. 14:36)? Surely these corrective outbursts assume that there is a more weighty principle that has been abused. They are corrective.

There are very few places today in the church where women are taking over or where peaceful fellowships have been marred by angry and militant women. But when one gets inside the depth of feeling that has been stirred, by both men and oppressive structures, I believe that women have deported themselves with more grace than the men who have failed to see the need for change. No one can liberate herself. And the day spent with the other sex must start with considering the challenge of loving the other half of the human race—certainly the other half of the church. It is a spiritual issue. It is also an equipping issue.

In *Liberating the Laity* I argue that ministry is more "caught" than "taught." The most important thing we can do toward equipping all the saints for ministry is to shape the environment in unity and complementarity so that every member "hears" from the environment the message: not *you*, but *we*; not your personal self-development, but building up the body as "each part does its work" (Eph. 4:16).[4] So we must discover what deep beliefs and values have shaped the present church environment so that women do not hear that *we* includes them. How is it possible that men could think that the body could be built up to the maturity of the stature of Christ without the female parts doing their work? What can be done to equip men and women to serve *together*?

A gracious conspiracy[5] is needed to equip women and men for full partnership in ministry. Women have roughly the same opportunities for training today as men, in Bible schools and seminaries, but most emerge to become second-class citizens, a new kind of laity-clergy distinction within the clergy itself. This has led some women to adopt an unnatural female *cum* male bearing or role. Perhaps in the past men in ministry frequently have denied or modified their masculinity in order to represent the whole church, male and female—thence my pastor's joke. The first step to address this situation is to find out why we are not listening to each other.

Talking Past Each Other

Reluctantly I have come to the conclusion that whether women teach, lead worship, become ordained, or become bishops is not in its essence a doctrinal issue. I am not alone in this conviction. Years ago Hendrik Kraemer commented:

> Behind these debates about disobedience or obedience to the divine Word there are, of course, hiding themselves also all the sociological and psychological inhibitions

which together build up the deeply entrenched masculine superiority assumption.[6]

1. It is a very personal issue. We come to the role of women in ministry out of extensive experience with the other sex and with biases and prejudices that are often too deep to verbalize. It would be a gift of God's Spirit to come to this subject with a truly teachable spirit, a gift for which we should pray.

Some come to the subject swept along by the tide of a secular movement pressing for "rights." Secular critiques of sex roles and authority types are applied to Scripture. The church is one more "target."

On the other extreme there are people within some churches who have placed tradition over Scripture and are so committed to their "interpretation of the Scripture" that no new light can come from God's Word. Michael Griffiths reports that he was once at a conference of Brethren in New Zealand when Jim Houston demolished most of the usual proof texts in support of male leadership. A male elder got to his feet and said, "Never mind all those verses; it's the principle that counts." Michael Griffiths concluded, "We were understandably speechless."[7] The price that has been paid for this deep prejudice is inestimable.

Florence Nightingale was an exceedingly gifted woman. Commenting on the church's openings for workers she wrote,

For women she has what? I had no taste for theological discoveries. I would have given her my head, my heart, my hands. She would not have them. She did not know what to do with them. She told me to go back and crochet in my mother's drawing room; or if I was tired of that, to marry and look well at the head of my husband's table. "You may go to the Sunday School, if you like it," she said. But she gave me no training even for that. She gave me neither work to do for her, nor education for it.[8]

On the other hand there are women and men who for years have obeyed what they believe is the Lord's clear direction that men should assume leadership and women should refrain from leadership, no matter how gifted and qualified either might be for the task. To suggest that a "new" interpretation of Scripture makes something formerly "wrong" into something "right" is spiritually confusing. This too is a matter of personal spirituality and one which challenges us with our willingness to allow the Scripture to speak freshly on subjects that are illuminated by the social forces in our own times. But there is more to this issue than merely personal spirituality and deep personal beliefs.

2. *It is a marriage issue.* People have carefully negotiated in the privacy of their home a settlement on the politics of marriage—usually with the husband as head, understood as ruler and decision-maker. It is everywhere attested that marriage should be upheld by the church, not only by its teaching but by its practice. This must include, so it is thought, not only the practice of covenant (my subject in *Married for Good*), but also in demonstrated male and female roles in the church. Many Christians fear that allowing women to lead, teach, and exercise a role with perceived authority, undermines the headship of husbands. Women will not be under men at home if men are under women at church, is the unspoken logic behind this fear. There is a half-truth involved here.

Husband and wife must never become merely marriage spouses with interchangeable roles and no gender distinctiveness. It is my conviction that the husband's headship must never be expressed as control or "decision-making authority." Headship is not control, and submission is not compliance. But there are spiritual reasons not to dissolve marriage into a mere spousal arrangement. Husband and wife play parts in a sacred drama, a mystery play in which we are acting out, in the nitty-gritty experience of our life together, something of the beauty of Christ's relationship with the church (Eph. 5:32). Paul does not spell out our job descriptions and roles, but describes the "spirit" of the marriage relationship and its spirituality—how it directs us to God, how it becomes a path to deeper life in God. In the sacred drama of each individual marriage we are free to write our own lines according to our personalities, but we do so knowing how the play ends—with the marriage supper of the Lamb—and knowing why we treasure sexual differences in marriage. Christians should be the last people on earth to abandon headship in marriage. They hold headship dear not because it preserves power and control for the male—in fact, it challenges the husband to empower his wife (Eph. 5:25-26)[9]—but because complementarity is the way we "play" this sacred drama called marriage. Not only ministry but marriage is in danger of being neutered today.

The solution for the marital confusion is not to enforce a ministry mandate that puts men over women in the church and home. Rather, we should rediscover complementarity in both the home and the church. And we should *live* it out incarnationally instead of institutionalizing the roles. That requires walking by faith (seeing the invisible) rather than sight (structuring the differences into visible gender-related job descriptions). But the next issue deepens the spiritual challenge of male-female mutual equipping in the church.

3. It is an authority issue. If women share with men in the *offices*, as well as the *functions* of ministry, will we not have a further undermining of the structures and symbols of authority everywhere threatened in Western society? The question betrays pre-Christian thinking.

We are called in Christ to experience and exercise a new kind of authority. Old Testament patterns of leadership cannot simply be applied to the New Testament church. It is sometimes said that because only males were priests in the Old Testament, only males can give visible leadership in the church today. But in the Letter to the Hebrews, Christ—not the elder or pastor—fulfills the priesthood of the former covenant. And in Christ all Christians—both men and women—share his superior priesthood in a priestly ministry that now includes all believers. Under the Old Testament, leadership included rule and decision-making authority. The reason for this is that only a few people knew the Lord in a personal way or had his Spirit in their hearts (Jer. 31:33-34). God did not have a "direct line" to all the members of his people. But under the New Covenant the authority of church leaders is a different matter.

Jesus said that the Gentiles rule and "lord it over them, and their high officials exercise authority over them. Not so with you" (Mark 10:42-43). The word which means "to domineer" is used only once in the New Testament, in 1 Timothy 2:12, where the women are forbidden to domineer the men. (Are not the men also forbidden by Paul to dominate the women?)[10] In Hebrews 13:17 the writer exhorts God's people to obey their leaders and to submit (or defer) to them. The NIV says "submit to their authority" but the last three words are significantly missing in the original. In Titus 2:15 Paul tells Timothy to "encourage and rebuke with all authority." The word used here *(epitage)* means "in accordance with the command you have" or "with all impressiveness." The usual word for "authority" *(exousia)* is used almost exclusively for the right and power of Jesus to decide and act, and for the unique leadership of his apostles. It is never used of one believer to make decisions for another or to have power over other members of the church. Nothing like a chain-of-command is implied or supported by the New Testament Scriptures either in marriage or in church leadership. In the church *the word* head *is never used for human leaders in the body of Christ*. Jesus is the head, period. Church leaders—whether male or female—do not have the right to command, but are called to equip the people to experience the headship of Jesus and to grow up into Christ, who is the head (Eph. 4:12, 15).

This does not mean that believers are without authority. As O. Betz says in his article in the *Theological Dictionary of the New Testament*:

> The authority of a Christian believer is founded on the rule of Christ and the disarming of all powers. It implies both freedom and service. As Luther put it in *The Freedom of a Christian*, "A Christian is a perfectly free lord of all, subject to none. A Christian is a dutiful servant of all, subject to all."[11]

If no believer has the right to make a decision for another believer (whether male or female), the authority issue is disarmed and refocussed. Whatever authority Christian leaders have, they have only in Christ and only for building others up (2 Cor. 10:8). Christ holds the ultimate authority. Leaders must equip members of the church to respond to the head for themselves. The process of equipping the saints to experience the authority and leadership of Jesus is something which will require both men and women in leadership, each contributing its sexual distinctiveness. The culture calls for parity or equivalency—equal opportunity and interchangeability. But the Bible calls for something much richer.

Synergistic Ministry

Medicine has an analogy for this: synergism. When two drugs are administered together, their effect is sometimes a multiple rather than a mere sum. When ministering leaders are men and women together, in ministering teams rather than males and females only (or worse still, androgynous facsimiles), their effect can be synergistic. In the light of Paul's rich affirmation by means of titles and personal greetings in Romans 16,[12] I cannot imagine Paul saying what I have heard from some of my male colleagues: "If you have the men in leadership, you will get the women too. Whereas, if you have the women, you may not get their husbands or their children."

The failure to equip the church for full partnership has been disastrous. Where only men are in ministry, they often have to develop an unnatural femininity in order fully to encompass the ministry of the church. This is particularly true of the one-man minister syndrome. Some women who have successfully broken into the male world of public ministry have succeeded only by adopting a masculine bearing. Is it not better for men to be men in ministry and leadership, and women to be women in ministry and leadership? I believe that is the main point Paul is making in the infamous passage in 1 Timothy 2:8, where he says, "I want men everywhere to lift up holy hands in prayer (implying as men), without anger or disputing" (the particular things that mar a man's public ministry), and, in verse 9, he says, "I also want women to dress modestly, with decency and propriety" (in other words, to worship as women, for the context is public worship).

The church has been neutered by the restriction of ministry roles to given genders, and by the resulting androgyny of her ministers. Speaking to this sexual poverty Jean Vanier notes,

I am convinced that our society desperately needs the reconciliation of men and women in order to build community together. . . . Women, for the most part, exercise authority differently from men, neither better nor worse. At certain times in the history of a community, it might be better to have a man carrying the responsibility; at other times a woman. The essential is that neither exercises authority alone. Woman has a need to lean on a man, and man on a woman.[13]

Aquila and Priscilla are good models of this divine syner-
gy. Their ministry together was greater than the sum of their
individual efforts. The wife, Priscilla, is named first more
often than the husband. Perhaps she was the natural leader
and Aquila was a big enough man to let his wife take the
lead if that was her gift. Their ministry was richer because
they were together.

God is not leading his new humanity into a sexless future,
or to a male hierarchical future, but to full and equal partnership as joint heirs and "fellow workers" (Rom. 16:3). If that is
where Christ is taking us, why would we want to take the
church back to a spoiled and cursed garden (Gen. 3:16) to put
women under men again?[14] I can understand men doing this,
for I am a man in process of liberation, but I cannot understand someone doing this as an act of worship to Christ, in
the name of Christ, the liberator and unifier.

In the last chapter I considered many of the biblical arguments for full partnership of men and women. Apparently
the Lord is not waiting for us to become convinced on the
cognitive level. God is obviously providing and equipping
women for leadership in the church. Ray Anderson is convinced that the resurrection of Jesus and the outpouring of
the Spirit on Pentecost demonstrates the Lord's way of inter-
preting the Scriptures. He concludes, "If Christ is at work
through his Holy Spirit setting apart women for pastoral
ministry with the evident blessing of God in their ministries,
then there will be full parity in pastoral ministry."[15] The effect
is synergistic. And the world is waiting to see such redeemed
sexuality and the full partnership of the sexes. The church is
in a position to model it, if only we would catch up to the
New Testament and follow the Lord as leader of his people.

9
Prayer and Sexuality

"The primitive impulse to deify sexual love was not wholly misguided. . . . "—Alan Ecclestone

"Marriage is, before it is anything else, an act of contemplation. It is a divine pondering, an exercise in amazement."—Mike Mason

Do sexuality and prayer belong together? These two ideas appear to be incongruous when placed alongside each other. Can we speak of prayerful sexuality, or sexual prayer? One has to do with wild appetites in the flesh—so it is thought—and the other with exalted spiritual life that is above the incessant demands of our physical existence. Unfortunately the church has been influenced for centuries by thinking that keeps these two realities apart.[1] In this final chapter on "A Day with the Other Sex," we will discover that bringing together prayer and sexuality is not only possible but vital for both married and single people.

In *Marriage Spirituality* I investigated spiritual disciplines *within* marriage—matters such as couple prayer, sharing solitude and doing God's will together. But there is an underlying assumption which I will draw out in this chapter. Marriage *itself* is a spiritual discipline.[2] We will also discover that the single life is also a spiritual discipline.

What makes a marriage an invitation to know God better is not that married life provides a *context* for religious activities as husband and wife. Rather, it is the *structure* of marriage itself—its constitution—that makes marriage Christian and an invitation to prayerfulness. In Matthew 19:4-6 and Ephesians 5:22-33, Jesus and Paul describe marriage as a radical, permanent covenant in which each lives for the other rather than self, in a relationship characterized by mutual submission. Two structural factors implicit in biblical marriage make marriage a path of response to God. First, there is the covenant foundation which links us with God's covenant with us. And second, there is the requirement of living together in mutual submission, which implicitly demands being filled continuously with the Holy Spirit. Both are an invitation to prayer.

The Covenant Foundation of Marriage

A covenant is a binding personal agreement to belong together permanently for the purpose of enriching each other's life. Though neither Jesus nor Paul use the word *covenant* when they speak of marriage, the relationship they describe is essentially covenantal. Both refer to the basic passage on the marriage covenant in Genesis 2:24. The covenant is made publicly (leaving father and mother), personally (being united in companionship) and privately (becoming one flesh). Marriage is total. It calls us out of ourselves and beyond ourselves. Mike Mason says that "marriage is to human relations what monotheism is to theology. It is a decision to put all the eggs in one basket, to go for broke, to bet all the marbles."[3] It is not surprising that many people today skip marriage and just live together, without realizing what they are missing.

Without understanding or wanting a covenantal marriage, many people opt for contractual arrangements in which "goods and services" are exchanged according to terms, usually unspoken. The contractual exchange may be worked out in terms of mutual emotional and sexual need-meeting.

When one party reneges on the terms, the other is free to leave. There is no "for better, for worse" in the terms! Many people in our society who have gone through a marriage ceremony do not actually get married in the covenantal sense. They may say the vows, but they have an emotional loophole "in case it doesn't work out." Entering marriage with the thought that one could leave it is to fail to enter it at all. A covenant is different.

Like God's covenant with Israel, and Christ's covenant with the bride (the church), the marriage covenant is an unconditional agreement to belong together "until death us do part." Its focus is not on doing but on being, not on performance but on belonging. The vows are deeply revelatory. We say, "I take you *to be* my wedded husband/wife. . . ." We do not say, "I take you *to do* . . . ." It is not surprising that most couples come to a church to say these vows. What is seldom appreciated is that the vows invite a lifelong marital prayer, not merely an initial prayer. There are theological reasons for this. We have a covenant-making and a covenant-keeping God.

Becoming a Christian can be understood in covenantal terms. Christ wooed us, courted us, and proposed marriage to us on behalf of the Father. By his death on the cross Christ cleared away every legal obstacle by which these two persons—a holy God and unworthy people—can belong together. To be invited into a covenant relationship means that God is more interested in being than in doing, more interested in relationship with us than in getting his work done on earth. Christ wants a spouse, not slaves. The appropriate response to his nuptial invitation is "I do." But we are not yet "married."

We are betrothed (2 Cor. 11:2). In New Testament times betrothal was a much more demanding agreement than is modern engagement. It was presexual marriage—the covenant without its consummation. So the marriage is not yet complete. But when Jesus comes again we will attend our own marriage (Rev. 19:7-9) and begin to spend eternity consummating our covenant relationship with Christ. The covenant is unconditional. But the blessings of the covenant are conditional on obedience, on living the lifestyle of the covenant people. When we fail to keep covenant, or when we break it, we bring pain on ourselves. But the covenant itself is never annulled. God will never divorce us. It is the same with the human facsimile: marriage.

The covenant itself is unconditional. The blessings of the covenant are conditional on showing faithfulness and love to one's spouse. No wonder we make vows! Promises are not good enough; they are too easily broken. When we cannot keep the vows, the vows "keep" us by calling us back to our true partner and inviting us to seek prayerfully the heart of our covenant God.

A pastoral counselor was talking with a man who was bound and determined to divorce his wife. The counselor asked him how he reconciled his position with the biblical mandate for husbands to love their wives. The man quickly replied, "After what she's done, I don't consider her to be my wife anymore!"

"Well then," the counselor replied, "she is still your neighbor, and the Bible says that we must love our neighbors."

After a moment's pause, the man replied, "I guess I don't really think that she's even my neighbor anymore!"

The counselor responded: "Well, then, you had better get serious about loving your enemy!"[4]

Some would say the covenant makes marriage a prison, but in reality it is a self-chosen monastery in which true freedom is found by pleasing the one we have chosen rather than endlessly looking for someone else to please us. In the process we are invited constantly to direct our love and prayers to our covenant-making and covenant-keeping God.

The Spirit-Filled Marriage

If covenant describes the relational structure of marriage, mutual submission describes the political structure of Christian marriage. It is seldom noted that in the familiar passage in Ephesians 5:18, "Be filled with the Spirit" is the main imperative in the section.[5] This is followed by another imperative that expresses *what the Spirit-filled life is like in crucial domestic relationships.* Verse 21 states the general principle: "Submit to one another out of reverence for Christ." The infallible indication that one is continuing to be inundated with the Spirit is one's hearty willingness to serve those closest in life by mutual submission.

Having established the principle of mutual submission, Paul then gives three relational contexts requiring the continuous inundation of the Holy Spirit to live the Christian life: husbands and wives (5:22-33), parents and children (6:1-4), and slaves and masters (6:5-9). Hardly ever does one hear a sermon or read an article that explains that the crucial sign of Spirit-filling is serving people that are close to us in life through mutual submission. Usually being filled with the Spirit is associated with ecstatic experiences rather than domestic graces.

In the spirit-filled marriage, the structure of power and powerlessness, control and compliance, has been replaced by the "politics" of mutual service. This is not easy. Mike Mason wisely reflects that marriage proposes an almost impossible degree of cooperation between two sovereign centers of personal will and power. Marriage is the assault of love on the castle of the ego. It is a "systematic program of deliberate and thoroughgoing self-sacrifice."[6] It invites prayer for the continuous transformation of our hearts. To make, keep, and fill one's marriage covenant is a spiritual ministry, and the failure to do this has spiritual implications.[7] Marriage is a path to God, rather than a distraction from holy living.[8] Marriage is a form of prayer, sometimes an acted prayer.

The Roman Catholic author Delores Leckey suggests that sexual intercourse is the ritual of the marriage covenant. She compared it to the communion bread and wine, physical elements through which we renew our promises to belong to God and revel in his promises never to forsake us. Similarly in the privacy of our bedrooms we renew, reaffirm, and deepen, in a very earthy and human way—as human as kneading bread and crushing grapes—the covenant-vows we made in public.[9]

Sexual intercourse is to married life what Sabbath is to work. It is a sacred pause that helps us make sense out of our marriage. Through the discipline of Sabbath we discover that our daily work is really work for God. Through the sexual embrace we remember that the details of our lives together are for love, and ultimately for God. In each case we return to the routine knowing why it is there.[10]

What makes marriage Christian and prayerful is not merely the presence of two Christians in the marriage relationship or even "having devotions together." Rather, it is two structural factors: the covenant, and Spirit-filled mutual submission. Both invite us to direct our attention toward God and to make our day with the other sex a day of prayer.

In exhorting husbands to love their wives and wives to respect their husbands (Eph. 5:21-33), Paul is not mainly giving a code of conduct for marriage. Each of the exhortations is conditioned with "out of reverence for Christ" (verse 21), "as to the Lord" (verse 22), and "as Christ" (verses 23, 25). These are statements about the way the Lord has designed marriage, even if one or both partners are not believers. They are statements about spirituality. God is already there, sown into the covenant relationship, waiting to be loved and served *through* our spouses as we submit to the grace of mutual submission. So in Christian marriage we do not merely try to find our fulfillment in marriage through the help of God, but find our fulfillment in God in the context of loving and serving our spouse. This subtle but important distinction—that God is the goal of marriage, and not merely personal satisfaction—becomes even clearer when we consider the discipline of singleness.

The Discipline of Singleness

While marriage is required for a complete sexual expression of covenant love, marriage is not a prerequisite for being sexually whole or for experiencing prayerful sexuality. Single people may still celebrate their appetite for covenant even while not allowing its full expression in the covenant of marriage. This can be true whether singleness is temporary or permanent, voluntary or involuntary. Richard Rohr, himself a single person, speaks to this prayerful celebration of sexuality. He believes that sexuality reveals something at the heart of reality and invites a spiritual response.

> God seemingly had to take all kinds of risks in order that we would not miss the one thing necessary: we are called and even driven out of ourselves by an almost insatiable appetite so that we would never presume that we were self-sufficient. It is so important that we know that we are incomplete, needy, and essentially social that God had to create a life-force within us that would not be silenced—not until 10 minutes after we were dead, they told us novices![11]

Complete satisfaction and fulfillment is not to found even in marriage. It is found in God. But is God enough for the single person? How can the single person relate prayer and sexuality?

Contemplative Singleness

One of my students at Regent College, herself single, expressed the connection between singleness and spirituality deeply and prophetically in a term paper. While affirming marriage, she offers her reflection on the grace of singleness. Prayer is crucial to this because it is the way we express our unity with the community of the Holy Trinity and mirror the harmony and beauty of that Trinitarian community. Singleness, she states, is reflected in the life of the Trinity.

Perhaps it is not too extravagant to suggest that within the functional and interwoven life of the Trinity is the quiet restfulness of contemplative embrace. Beyond all action is the potential of Sabbath rest and life entirely abandoned to the love and care of God. Certainly Sabbath contentment is *not* solely or exclusively a gift for the single person, but realistically singleness presents fewer hindrances to such an experience of God than does the married state. However, for the single person, as for the married, it is only as an individual attains maturity as a sexual being and learns to order his or her sexuality that authentic contentment will ever be possible. Contentment in singleness, contentment with celibacy, is equally the vehicle of divine love, but it, too, requires a realistic and healed understanding of sexuality.[12]

She proposes that prayer is the way not only to "tame" our sexuality, but to find God through it. Our sexual longings are an invitation to prayer.

It is in prayer that we are called to seek, through honest and transparent communion with the Father, the proper ordering of our sexual life. It is the Father, who in ever deepening relationship with us, teaches us our own way of being in the world and leads us into appropriate and healthy relationships. It is the Father who will teach us how to live as sexual beings with deep creational needs for union and intimacy within a celibate state, and ultimately it will be the Father who transforms the occasional sense of isolation into rich and unhurried experience of fruitful solitude alone with Him.[13]

For most singles some parallel or substitute for marriage is needed to accomplish such a mature integration of prayer and sexuality. Christian communities, house groups, intentional living communities, Christian orders, teams of missionaries, and partnerships of people working on similar societal ministries, provide a relational context to experience companionship and to share the human journey in all of its richness. Special friendships—like David and Jonathan's friendship[14]—are a very precious gift, especially when each can help the other "find strength in God" (1 Sam. 23:16). It is especially tragic that in Western society same-sex friendships, such as that of David and Jonathan, are soiled with sexual suspicion. There need be nothing sinful in a healthy friendship. Christians must dare to live counterculturally, not being intimidated by the perverted minds around them.

Having said this, we must conclude that even "special friends" will not meet all the needs of single people, and, contrary to what is commonly believed, married people have relational needs that cannot be completely satisfied by their spouses. Whether single or married, we were intended to live as sexual and prayerful people in a new humanity composed of men and women who follow Jesus—the people of God. Our sexual appetite cries for community, a community experiencing cohumanity (Gen. 1:27) and sexual complementarity. So the "Day with the Other Sex" invites the consideration of our next subject, "a Day with Brothers and Sisters."

PART FOUR

A DAY WITH BROTHERS AND SISTERS

10
Relational Spirituality

"Can human beings be persons today? Can a man be his actual self with another man or woman?"—R. D. Laing

"God is friendship, and whoever abides in friendship abides in God."—Aelred of Rievaulx

"Anyone without a soul friend is a body without a head."
  Celtic Saying

Unquestionably my primary theological education has been from *people*, not books or classes. And the history of my own spiritual life is substantially the history of my relationships: my mother and father, whom I can still see kneeling beside their bed nightly to pray for me; Fred Daubert, a young man in university residence who walked with me through my first confusing days as a Christian; my wife, Gail, who has taught me more through her prayers than by her words; my next-door neighbor in Montreal, a Roman Catholic who opened my heart to different Christian spiritualities; the late Dennis Clark, who encouraged me to pay the price of being unconventional, and my present supervisor, Walter Wright, who has demonstrated the beauty of exalting the ministry of others. I have also learned some disturbing things about myself through reflecting on my relational history: I have discovered that I am more controlling than I care to admit.

Many Christians are either relationally starved or relationally addicted. At the same time—as we discovered in the last chapter—we have deep relational needs that can be substantially satisfied by our brothers and sisters in the family of God. This relational hunger—both in its healthy and unhealthy expressions—is a spiritual issue and an opportunity for spiritual formation. In these three chapters the disciplines of our hungry hearts will focus on our life together, but with a difference.

Our approach will involve exploring the biblical theme of the people of God as a royal priesthood (1 Pet. 2:9). In Christ the whole believing community, not merely its leaders, has become a vehicle for the Lord's ministry. Priests touch people and places for God, showing God's grace and purpose to others. They also "touch" God through intercessory prayer on behalf of people and places—a two directional priesthood. In this chapter we will explore this two-way ministry in our relational life in the people of God. Peter said, "Once you were not a people (the Greek word is *laos* or laity), but now you are the people of God" (1 Pet. 2:10). The transformation from not belonging and not having an identity, to belonging and knowing who we are, involves three relational transformations.

From Service to Friendship

Consciously or unconsciously most relationships we form with brothers and sisters serve our own interests. This is not all wrong, but in its extreme form it is expressed as relational addiction: We need people to fill up the insatiable emptiness within. The psychiatrist R. D. Laing expressed this: "We are effectively destroying ourselves by violence masquerading as love."[1] He further reflects, "No wonder modern man is addicted to other persons and the more addicted, the less satisfied, the more lonely."[2] The bottom line of this relational pathology is that relationships exist only *to serve us*. Ironically, the result of self-serving relationships is deep loneliness and friendlessness, because friendship is not *for* anything at all.

Speaking to this, Simone Weil said, "Friendship is a miracle by which a person consents to view from a certain distance, and without coming any nearer, the very being who is necessary to him as food."[3] She said, "A friendship is tarnished as soon as necessity triumphs, if only for a moment, over the desire to preserve the faculty of free consent on both sides."[4] Jesus addressed this fundamental reality in his own relationship with the disciples. He insisted "I no longer call you servants, because a servant does not know his master's business. Instead I have called you friends" (John 15:15). I find these words among the most remarkable in the New Testament, and profoundly challenging to the spiritual life. Most people want to be servants of Christ—or want Christ to be their servant—but Jesus wants to become our friend.

Even within the twelve friends, Jesus had closer friendship with Peter, James, and John, who were invited to be with him on the Mount of Transfiguration, the healing of Jairus' daughter, and in the Garden of Gethsemane. John came to be known as "the disciple whom Jesus loved" (John 21:20). It is a testimony to the purity of his friendship with Peter and James, and especially with John that the others seemed not to be jealous of that. If Jesus moved from a service relationship to friendship, those who are priests in Jesus will do the same. But why is building friendship *a priestly ministry* that touches people for God and God for people?

In his classic, *Spiritual Friendship*, the twelfth-century Cistercian monk Aelred of Rievaulx wrote that friendship between believers is a direct path to God, not a diversion from it. He boldly paraphrases 1 John 4:16: "God is friendship, and whoever abides in friendship abides in God." It is a provocative thought. Is there something in the Trinity of God that can truly be called friendship, something beyond mutual usefulness and service? Does the Father love the Son

(John 17:23-24, 26), not for what the Son will do for him, but for the Son himself—the pure enjoyment and appreciation of another? Is this the deepest meaning of the love mandate of Jesus: "As the Father has loved me, so have I loved you. Now remain in my love" (John 15:9)? Are we touching people for God most when we least intend to do something for them, or to get them to do what we want, but, rather, when we treat them as friends? Aelred describes a spiritual friend as someone

> to whom you dare to speak on terms of equality as to another self, one to whom you need have no fear to confess your failings; one to whom you can unblushingly make known what progress you have made in the spiritual life; one to whom you can entrust all the secrets of your heart and before whom you can place all your plans.[5]

This insight did not come to Aelred through books, but was wrung out of the suffering of his own life. Aelred's youth included habitual sexual sin with other men. His victory over this led him both to condemn homosexual activity as an especially direct road to hell and, at the same time, to continue to believe in tenderness, affection, touching, being open, and talking intimately about one's life. Unlike the more extreme desert fathers, Aelred dealt with the fear of sex in an all-male world by insisting that warm love between friends of the same sex could be pure.[6] He underwent a lifelong process of conversion to this. It may be the same for us.

Aelred captured, possibly better than any other, the essence of relational priesthood. Friendship, as described by Aelred, is not a *condition* for ministry; it *is* ministry. When we listen to the heart, when we renounce our own agendas for the person, when we refuse to play God in another's life, when we discern the movement of God, when we appreciate the unique spirituality of a friend, when we explore the questions a friend is asking, when we nurture another's life in God, when we keep a confidence, and when we leave our friend dependent on God rather than ourselves, we are priests of Jesus Christ.

Our utilitarian society makes friendship difficult. It invites us to become relational prostitutes by "making friends" in order to minister. So we *use* friendship as a relational bridge, especially in what is called friendship evangelism. But what if the "friend" does not become a Christian? Do we drop him or her? If we did, we would be proving that we have not made a friendship at all. Friendship is not *for* anything. It is uncalculating. In a sense, it is useless.[7] Is it possible that we *only* minister to those who are our friends, and that the record of our friendships is the record of our spiritual pilgrimages?

James Houston speaks of the interrelationship of our spiritual life with friendships:

A true friend can never have a hidden motive for being a friend. He can have no hidden agenda. A friend is simply a friend, for the sake of friendship. In a much greater way, love for God is love for God's own sake. Bernard of Clairvaux wrote that our natural inclination is to love for our own sake. When we learn to love God, we still love him for our own sake. As we grow in friendship with God, we come to love him not just for ourselves alone, but also for God's sake. At last, we may reach a point where we love even ourselves for the sake of God.[8]

But we must now consider a second priestly movement that is equally countercultural.

From Criticism to Intercession

One of the most formative experiences in my wife's spiritual pilgrimage happened on a Pioneer Camp canoe trip as a teenager. Two of the girls were criticizing a third. But the counselor, a spiritually sensitive woman, said, "Have you considered that God has given us a spirit of discernment not to criticize but to pray?" Touché. Priests are people who progressively relinquish their tendency to assassinate the character of others verbally—either directly or indirectly in their absence—in order to *touch God on their behalf through prayer.* Priesthood, we have recognized, is both touching people and places for God, and touching God on behalf of people and places. Intercession is one of the deepest ministries of the Christian priest.

Intercessory prayer is hard work (Eph. 1:15-23; 3:14-21). It is hard to hold people in our hearts and then to take them to God in our praying hearts. But the ministry of Scripture at this point is not so much to tell us how to pray, as to show us what happens when we do. On the subject of prayer the Bible is much more concerned with "how come?" than with "how to," especially the last book of the Scripture.

Revelation does not exhort us to pray, but rather evokes prayer by revealing the one to whom we pray. It is an appeal to the faith of beleaguered saints in all centuries by means of the imagination. The vision of the Lamb on the throne, of incense and smoke, together with the prayers of the saints going up before God from the hands of a mighty angel and a heaven that responds with thunder, rumblings, flashes of lightning, and an earthquake (Rev. 8:4-5), and even more eloquently by half an hour of silence (8:1), is enough to empower the weakest intercessor to pray. The impact of Revelation is not simply the conviction that prayer works. Prayer does not work if it is calculated by cost-effectiveness or technological efficiency; indeed, judged by these standards it is sheer waste. But consider what intercessory prayer does in our journey out of ourselves toward God and his purposes with other people.

Calculated from the perspective of the New Jerusalem, some very important things happen when we pray for others. First, we gain God's mind and perspective about the person we are holding before God. Second, we piggy-back on the Spirit's intercession for that person since our prayers, even the most eloquent ones, are mere groans and babblings in comparison to the eloquence of the Spirit (Rom. 8:26). Third, in some mysterious way that offends the secular mindset, we get in touch with that person on a deeper level than we might otherwise. Bonhoeffer explains this in these terms: Direct relationships between people are impossible. But Jesus as our mediator puts his hand on each and brings both together. So the most direct way to our brother is indirect—through Christ. "Christ stands between us, and we can only get into touch with our neighbors through him. That is why intercession is the most promising way to reach our neighbors."[9]

Finally, *something happens* when we pray for people. Pascal said that "prayer is God's way of providing man with the dignity of causality."[10] P. T. Forsyth agrees that the earth is shaken daily by the prayers of the saints: "The real power of prayer in history is not a fusillade of praying units of whom Christ is the chief, but it is the corporate action of a Savior-Intercessor and His community, a volume and energy of prayer organized in a Holy Spirit and in the Church the Spirit creates. The saints shall thus judge the world and control life."[11] So Christian priests pray. They pray because God the Holy Spirit and Jesus the Son pray. And they join these prayers on behalf of others. But there is a further priestly ministry that lines the believer up with the intentions of God.

From Independence to Accountability

One of the last "rights" to be relinquished in our atomized, individualistic society is our independence. It makes priesthood relationally impossible. To grow in Christ or serve him well in the world we will have to live interdependently. Mutual submission is the centerpiece of the Christian life

(Eph. 5:21). In the church it is not self-interest, but looking to the interests of others that builds up the body. This mutual care and accountability works best if we invite others to function as our priests in very specific ways.

In 1738 John Wesley provided questions to be asked of those seeking admission to the band meetings:

> Do you desire to be told your faults? . . . and that every one of us should tell you, from time to time, whatsoever is in his heart concerning you? Do you desire that, in doing this, we should come as close as possible, that we should cut to the quick?[12]

At every class meeting the members were asked what sins they had committed since the previous meeting and even what temptations and thoughts they had experienced.

Perhaps the radical surgery prescribed by Wesley is not appropriate for every fellowship, but his recommendation challenges an important myth: the idea of a "pure" fellowship. Tragically, there is often no place for a sinner in the church. As Bonhoeffer says,

> He who is alone with his sin is utterly alone. . . . The final breakthrough to fellowship does not occur, because, though they have fellowship with one another as believers and as devout people, they do not have fellowship as the undevout, as sinners. The pious fellowship permits no one to be a sinner. So everybody must conceal his sin from himself and from the fellowship. We dare not be sinners. Many Christians are unthinkably horrified when a real sinner is suddenly discovered among the righteous. We remain alone without sin, living in lies and hypocrisy. The fact is that we *are* sinners![13]

Undoubtedly the tragic downfall of several outstanding Christian leaders in recent years could have been avoided if they had belonged to a real fellowship in which there was mutual confession and mutual submission. But we must ask why some dark, demon inside us resists this priestly ministry of others so fervently. Kefa Sempangi, who was nurtured in the East Africa Revival, offers a clue: "We are too proud to give our lives away to people who are not perfect."[14] What grace we can experience if we do.

Three priestly ministries. The first two—friendship and intercession—call forth in ourselves a deeper life in God as we reach out to become relational priests to our brothers and sisters. But the third movement—towards mutual submission—explicitly adds a further dimension: equipping others to become *our priests*. All three taken together serve to release the mutual ministry of brothers and sisters and to recover the people of God as a royal priesthood. Adapting an adage first uttered by John R. Mott, it is better to get ten people to become priests than to do the priestly work of ten people.

11
Mutuality

"The priesthood of all believers can be lost in a single generation."—Oscar Feuchts

"Sir, you wish to serve God and go to heaven? Remember that you cannot serve him alone. You must therefore find companions or make them; the Bible knows nothing of solitary religion."—"Serious Man" to John Wesley

We lost three family members in one year: my mother and father, and Gail's only brother, Garth. It was a year we needed the priesthood of all believers. Various people from the church came to the door and offered their encouragement. Some chattered; some told stories about their own bereavements; some did not know what to do but came anyway. We were grateful for every initiative and felt deeply loved. But one couple touched us especially. They met us at our door with tears in their eyes, saying very little, drawing us out, listening with their hearts, weeping with us. "Tell us more about what it is like." And we poured out our feelings. When they left, we felt that God had been listening.

That night, reflecting on the day's mourning, Gail and I turned to 2 Corinthians 1:3-4, which speaks of the "God of all comfort, who comforts us in all our troubles, so that we can comfort those in any trouble with the comfort we ourselves have received from God." Suddenly we had a thought. Does God comfort us by listening—just like our friends from the church? Does God speak his comfort, not by speaking words of encouragement, but with his ears, through his silence?

The following Sunday a young member of our church ministered to us as a family. Jeff Spruston had been in and out of our home for years as part of our children's circle of friends. But in the middle of the service Jeff stood up and said, "The Stevens have ministered to us; now it is our turn to minister to them. Please join me while I pray for them." And, as a true priest, he prayed right into my heart and touched me for God. For that is what a priest does.

Misunderstanding Priesthood

The Protestant doctrine of the priesthood of all believers is a precious and life-giving doctrine, but it can be lost in a single generation. It has almost been lost in ours. It has been co-opted by the granular individualism of Western culture, making it essentially a do-it-yourself, individual priesthood, instead of the corporate priesthood of *all* the people of God. But more serious still, the priesthood of all the people of God has been clericalized. When priesthood is understood exclusively as handling and touching religious things and performing overtly religious activities (such as leading worship or teaching a Bible study), it gets restricted to the gathered life of the church and one's discretionary time, except for the full-time professional. In reality no part-time priesthood is available for the people of God. If you are in Christ, you are in the priesthood (1 Pet. 2:9-11; Rev. 1:6). So a day with brothers and sisters—whether in the church or the world—is a day of giving and receiving ministry, mutual priesthood.

Recovering Interdependence

I had a vision one day while our church was worshipping. As I looked around at the people I have come to love, I saw that each was an earthen vessel, a real mud pot. I knew this picture was authentic by the test of Scripture (2 Cor. 4:7). But as I continued to look, in prayer and worship, I looked "into" each mud pot, and what I saw was exquisite molten gold. Each person, frail, vulnerable, and half-fashioned, had a treasure inside. But then I saw something more—each pot was cracked. Finally I looked again and saw something miraculous: the molten gold was oozing through the cracks. That is how ministry comes into the world, not poured out of expensive vases, but through the orifice of the faults and weaknesses of real people who are being transfigured by Christ. But there is a problem with this vision.

No one is in Christ alone. No one ministers alone. All ministry is mutual, reciprocal, and interdependent. As Paul suggests in Ephesians 4:16, we cannot "join" the church as one would join a club. Rather we are "joints" in the body. The word sometimes translated "joints" (PHILLIPS) or "ligaments" (NIV) in Ephesians 4:16 does not mean that certain members of the body have the special charisma of making all the connections for others. I once thought this was the pastor's job, but I am now convinced otherwise. The root meaning suggests "touch" or "contact." Paul is saying that every member *in his or her contact with other members* supplies something the body needs. Markus Barth translates this verse: "He (Christ) provides sustenance to it through every contact."[1] The Christian life is a life of social solidarity and true love for God and neighbor.

As God-imagining creatures, relational life is not a mere accessory to spirituality or ministry, but the heart of it. Finding unity within diversity because of the diversity, and not in spite of it, is an important link with the unity within God himself and is both a mark of spirituality and true ministry.

The word *together* appears so frequently in Paul's writings that it deserves special study. Paul uses the Greek prefix *sun* ("with" or "together") and joins this prefix to a number of key words to describe the practical impossibility of being in Christ alone. What is translated into English as a phrase is one compound word in the original: "fellow citizens with God's people" (Eph. 2:19); "joined together" (2:21); "being built together" (2:22); and, reaching a climax, "joined and held together by every supporting ligament" (4:16). Paul is using the strongest possible language—indeed he is creating new language—to describe the interdependence of every member of the body. We can no more disconnect ourselves from other members and remain healthy than we can disconnect the ligaments from the bones or try to live without veins or arteries. But undoubtedly the greatest challenge is to discover the mutual priesthood of two identified parts of the church: the clergy and the laity.

Recovering Lay Priesthood

The word *laity* is a word that needs redefining. In biblical language it is a term of incredible honor. It means "the people of God." Once we were not a people at all, but now in Christ we have become the laity of God (1 Pet. 2:10). A pastor or Christian workers cannot rise to a higher honor than being a member of God's laity! But in common speech *layperson* means untrained, unqualified, and not an expert. The Greek word for "unqualified" and "not an expert" is never used by an inspired apostle to describe the Christian believer. Ironically, *kleros*, the word from which we derive *clergy*, means "appointed" and "those who have received an inheritance" and is used for all the people of God who have received an inheritance in Christ (Eph. 1:11; Col. 1:12; Gal. 3:29). So the New Testament envisions a people who have no "laypersons" in the usual sense of the word, and yet is composed entirely of clergy, in the true sense of that word! How can we begin to actualize this magnificent biblical truth?

When I met with my class in Africa I had a bright idea. Why not let the laypeople teach the pastors, the reverse of the usual way? The most precious resource we had in this group of leaders in a rapidly growing denomination in Africa was the people who thought they had come to be equipped as "lay pastors." But equipping the saints for the work of the ministry (Eph. 4:11-12) does not mean training laypeople to assist the pastor in the pastor's ministry. Just the reverse; it means equipping all the people of God so that pastors will assist laypeople in the release of their ministry in everyday life: work, family, neighborhood, church, and nation. Who is better equipped to express the need for this than the laypeople themselves?

We had in the class a forestry official, an inspector for the Kenya pension fund, a school teacher, a manager of a small restaurant, two homemakers, a school bursar, and a businessperson who manufactures tables and caskets. We divided the class into small groups with one of our lay priests in each group as the resource person. Each group had to discuss three questions with their lay leader: First, what are the issues you face in your daily work? Second, what difference does your faith make to how you handle these issues? Third, what can the church do to help equip you for your full-time ministry as a servant of Christ on the job? The effect was electric.

Grace and Virginia work with women, the backbone of Africa. The list of problems they deal with is overwhelming: illiteracy, overwork, poor communication with their husbands, homes that are in reality only houses, favoritism of certain children in the home, crises between in-laws, misunderstanding about contraception ("Most people," they say, "take it as their responsibility 'to fill the earth' "), and separation from husbands. Frequently the men work in Nairobi and, for lack of funds, come home only once a month to visit their wives and children on the shamba/farm. Having taken up with a prostitute or a female friend in Nairobi, they may bring AIDS to their wives. "But it is impossible for these wives to refuse their husbands!" And so the dreaded plague spreads. But Grace and Virginia are full-time "priests" to women as they try to understand their situation from the perspective of God's Word and take appropriate steps to empower the women of Kenya.

John Njihia is a carpenter who runs a small shop in Nairobi. He encounters a thousand problems: workers steal materials; some of his staff are inefficient; customers refuse to pay when the work is complete; even some Christians want to be bribed. John's faith is at work in the shop on Monday, and not just on Sunday: he finds himself motivated to counsel the unemployed who come to him seeking work. Sometimes he is able to pray with customers. He feels he can stand firm with Jesus in a complex world.

In our class of thirty there grew an amazing unity between those who were ordained and those whose primary ministry is in society. *They became one people.* I became convinced that theological education must be for the whole people of God, and not just pastors. Further, I became convinced that the clergy need to receive some of their theological education from the rest of the people of God.[2] As pastors asked these laypeople to share their faith, and to share how the church could work with them to turn their jobs into fulltime ministry, I wondered, *Why are pastors in North America not inviting their laypeople to become equippers of the pastors? And what will it take for pastors and non-pastors in my own country to become mutual priests?*

12
Embodied Love

"Our gifts are on loan. We are responsible for spending them in the world."—Elizabeth O'Connor

"The world is anything but ready for a revival of Christian materialism. It is more ready for a revival of religion, of course, but religion and Christianity are by no means the same thing."—Robert Farrar Capon

If priesthood is touching the world and people *for* God, then our daily work is one vehicle through which God touches the earth and keeps his world running his way. Whether we are keeping business accounts, assembling cars on the line, or functioning as a homemaker, we are working for God and for others. As the apocryphal Book of Ecclesiasticus put it, workers keep "stable the fabric of the world." The quotation comes from an inspiring, though not inspired, book, and is worth quoting at length:

> How can he become wise who handles the plow . . . who drives oxen and is occupied with their work, and whose talk is about bulls? He sets his heart on plowing furrows, and he is careful about fodder for his heifers. So too every craftsman and master craftsman who labors by night as by day; those who cut the signets of seals, each is diligent in making a great variety; he sets his heart on painting a life-like image, and he is careful to finish his work. So too

is the smith sitting by the anvil, intent upon his handiwork in iron. . . . So too is the potter sitting at his work and turning the wheel with his feet; he is always deeply concerned over this world. He molds the clay with his arm and makes it pliable with his feet; he sets his heart to finish the glazing, and he is careful to clean the furnace. All these rely upon their hands, and each is skillful in his own work. Without them a city cannot be established, and men can neither sojourn nor live there. . . . *They keep stable the fabric of the world, and their prayer is the practice of their trade.* (Ecclesiasticus 38:25-32, RSV, emphasis mine)

The last sentence is highly suggestive of both priestly movements. The upward movement is *blessing God through our work, making it a prayer.* The "downward" movement is "keeping stable the fabric of the world," or touching the world for God.[1] Luther was eloquent on this subject. How else could God get the cows milked than through the labor of milkmaids? The shepherds who visited the Christ-child in the manger did not return to a monastery, but to their flocks, because that was their spiritual ministry.[2] But there is more to priesthood than merely doing our daily work with the intention of pleasing God. To explore the "worldly" dimension of the priesthood of all believers I will consider three priestly movements that concern space, time, and information.[3]

From Space to Place

Adam was placed in an undeveloped park—space—and instructed to take care of it, cultivate it, and develop it into a place.[4] Adam and Eve were the first homemakers, the first environmental engineers, the first theologians *of place.* The Bible is concerned about place, and not merely space. Jesus regarded place important enough to go ahead of us to prepare a place for each of us (John 14:2). Though Adam's successors created the first city in their sinful revolt (Gen. 4:17), the city is not an innately evil place. In the end we will all be city-dwellers. In the final insemination of this world by the kingdom of God in the last day, all remaining space will become place (Rev. 21:2) in the Holy City. There will be no more nameless expanses and no canned environments. Jesus does not go ahead to prepare a hotel room, or a nameless campground space with a number. His ministry is place-making. So is ours.

In much smaller ways, but in ways that make our daily work into something holy, we share in the priesthood of Jesus in creating place.[5] I remember moving into our first home and finding it to be space without place: six empty rooms that echoed with our excited voices as we took up occupancy. But it had no significant boundaries, no shape that we could call our own. So we took off the old green wooden shutters, painted the walls, sanded the floors, moved in some furniture, created a study area, pulled out the old cupboards, and made a house into a home. In the same way worker-priests in the marketplace, parents in the home, and leaders in the church create place out of space.

Don Flow runs an automotive dealership. He is active in his local church, but his main ministry is in the workplace. As a worker-priest he believes he must create a *gracious* place for his employees and his customers. Even though many of his employees are not followers of Jesus, he has developed a mission that captures all his staff with the challenge of creating a community where people are prized, where people will have the opportunity to grow and mature, and where customers will be treated with utmost respect and fairness. He is determined to give his customers "extraordinary service," knowing all along that the Greek word for "service" is the same word as "ministry." So he motivates his employees to engage in a full-time *ministry* to their customers. To accomplish this creation of place he has, on occasion, put on his overalls and joined the cleaners in their work. No one has bothered to ordain him to this priesthood, but he knows himself to be called to this ministry.

In the church priests engage in the same spiritual movement: from space to place. Many local churches are spaces in the city with no welcoming place. Many members go to a building every Sunday but feel they have no place that they can call their own. The family pew—once purchased—is now gone. Perhaps that is a good thing, as it tended to exclude visitors and outsiders. But the important place of emotional and spiritual at-homeness is significantly missing. Making church-space into church-place is a ministry for all the believers, not just the pastor. But priesthood is concerned with time as well as space.

From Clock Time to Significant Time

When Jesus says that the kingdom of God is within you (Luke 17:21), he gives a powerful hint that eternity can irrupt into ordinary time. The New Testament uses two different words to express the complexity of our experience of time. Ordinary time or clock time is *chronos*. We derive the word *chronological* from this Greek word. It is time that goes on and on. There is always too much or too little *chronos* for Western people. *Chronos* is easily organized. But the New Testament uses the word *kairos* for those times fraught with hope, meaning, opportunity, and eternal consequences. *Kairos* is the time of salvation (Mark 1:15), the time that evokes faith and calls for wisdom (Col. 4:5), the time in which God draws near, the accepted time (2 Cor. 6:2), the time of judgment (1 Pet. 4:17), transcendent time.[6] A dull lecture goes on and on—*chronos*—until the professor announces a short and unexpected test—*kairos*. The priest knows the difference.

Parents desperately want quality time with their children in this frenetic society, so they organize "quality" time. A cartoonist once said that quality time is what parents give to children when they do not have quantity time to give to them. But these "quality" time events may be spent in chilly silence, or the parents, being preoccupied with their own planning and concerns, are not even present with their own children. It is *chronos*. Quality time—as something scheduled and organized into the date book—is a myth. But one day as father leaves to attend an important business meeting, his daughter asks, "Dad, what is so wrong about premarital sex?" and he must choose whether or not to accept the gift of *kairos*. "Quality" time sometimes irrupts when quantity time is given with faith and expectancy.

Priesthood is concerned especially with *kairos*, waiting for it, expecting it, praying for it, discerning it, and embracing it. It is God who turns *chronos* into *kairos*, so giving us hope, opportunity, and, as we shall see in the chapters on Sabbath, deep rest.

The experience of *kairos* reminds us that our dominion over time is limited. We can and should present all the time of our lives as an offering to God. Madeleine L'Engle says that *kairos* is that real time that "breaks through *chronos* with a shock of joy, that time we do not recognize while we are experiencing it, but only afterwards."[7] *Kairos* is uncontrollable. So priests need to be ready with a word from God in season and out of season (2 Tim. 4:2), but they must learn to discern the "in season" moments. Usually confronting someone involved in an inappropriate romance falls on deaf ears. Counseling when help is not requested, preaching *at* a brother or sister, and giving spiritual direction to someone who is not ready to be nudged toward God, are often forced attempts to make *chronos* into *kairos*. They almost always fail. We may win the argument, and lose our brother or sister. So priests wait for this gift with their brothers and sisters just as a very sick person waits for the morning light, or an expectant woman waits for her moment of delivery. And God does not disappoint us because he is Lord of time.

From Information to Mystery

This third priestly ministry is especially important in this information age, when words are processed, digitalized, and packaged. We need priests who will work on the edge of mystery. I found this out the hard way.

I was almost ready to boast that I had produced my first sermon on my new word processor when I pushed the wrong button. Not having any rough notes, nor having saved anything along the way, twenty pages of words disappeared from the screen, never to be retrieved. There was not even a wave-form left in the chips of the deep memory. My words were gone like my sins in the blood of Christ! But the experience was deceiving.

Understood biblically, a person's words are not mere bits of information stored in a computer, wave-forms in a computer chip, or assemblages on a screen that can be dispatched with a misdirected finger. Words are expressions of the inner person and bear the vitality of the person who speaks them. Behind the word is the person who spoke it. Jesus himself said something similar, that the mouth speaks out of the heart (Matt. 12:34). If a person's words "fall to the ground" and have no impact, it is probably because they come from a superficial person. God's Word, in contrast, never returns to him empty (Isa. 45:23; 55:11).

Understood Hebraically, the person comes out of the mouth; we literally speak ourselves. So there is a mystery to be encountered whenever someone speaks. It is commonplace to say that there is more to a communication than the mere words, but we say this partly because in our culture we are devaluing words, and therefore we devalue the people who communicate themselves through their words. The priesthood of all believers includes this great relational reversal: We listen to people (not just words) and we hold people in awe. Robert Capon says, "The work of theology in our day is not so much interpretation as contemplation. . . .

God and the world need to be held up for *oohs* and *ahhs* before they can be safely analyzed. Theology begins with admiration, not problems."[8] If this is the work of theology, then the work of spirituality is to hold people up for *oohs* and *ahhs* when we encounter them in the church or the marketplace and at home.

This Earthy Love

We are hardly ready for the priesthood of place, time, and mystery. For many Christians it is not "spiritual" enough, and too down-to-earth. We have forgotten our original parents, the shape of our salvation, and the destiny we embrace in the New Jerusalem.

The priesthood of Adam and Eve in the garden was an embodied ministry—naming, cultivating, integrating, releasing potential, envisioning, creating. Our down-to-earth God literally came down to earth. The Incarnation is either the supreme religious embarrassment or the most exquisite expose about the transcendent meaning of the daily round. If the Word became flesh (John 1:14) cosmically, physically, personally, aesthetically, spiritually, and eternally, then ordinary life has meaning. God can go no farther to show us. If God makes wine for a wedding reception and crafts cribs for Nazarene babies, then we had better rethink holiness and priesthood. Prayer for the Christian has everything to do with the here and now. All work, whether artistic, mental or manual, when done for God in faith, is a joy to God, an acted prayer, embodied holiness, a priestly movement. The ordinary is extraordinary for the Christian priest. If, as Ecclesiasticus says, "their prayer is in the practice of their trade," it is a very earthy way of praying. If the Incarnation is true, then Christian spirituality does not merely encourage prayer *while one works* but rather *the work itself becomes prayer,* a much bigger thing. Perhaps it is even a better thing.

PART FIVE

A DAY
ALONE

13
Disciplines of the Hungry Heart

"To have found God and still to pursue Him is the soul's paradox of love, scorned indeed by the too-easily-satisfied religionist, but justified in happy experience by children of the burning heart."
—A.W. Tozer

"Every man who delights in a multitude of words, even though he says admirable things, is empty within. If you love truth, be a lover of silence."—St. Isaac of Nineveh

Why do you pray so much?" I asked this question of a pastor who rises at four to pray for three or four hours.

"It's a matter of survival," he replied. "I'm desperate."

Equally needy is the stockbroker whose ministry brings him into engagement with the principalities and powers of the financial world. Spiritual disciplines *are* born of desperation. We should think of ourselves as swimming in a stream to save our lives. In our society our identities are shaped from the outside rather than the inside: by what we know, what we do, what we possess, where we have been, what we have accomplished, and who we know. The day alone is the creation of an intended opportunity to allow our identity to be shaped from the inside. The spiritual life, as von Hugel points out, is not a circle revolving around a single point of ascetic detachment, but "an ellipse round two centers: detachment and attachment."[1] Walter Hilton called this "the mixed life," and it is the detachment part of the mixed life we are exploring.

Until now we have been speaking of "disciplines" as life-paths. Work, family, marriage, singleness, and the fellowship of believers are spiritual disciplines because they invite contemplation and prayerfulness. But in these three chapters we are exploring some of the specific responses we may make to the seeking Father in "A Day Alone." Our need is greater than we realize.

We are persecuted people. Our souls are being raped by the media. The places where a person can escape entertainment get fewer every day. A trip to the dentist no longer involves a brief reflective encounter with personal pain; we are soothed by watching a favorite program on a TV overhead. Canned music floats through tiny speaker holes in the ceilings of elevators. Advertising experts tell us that the average North American is exposed to about 1200 advertisements every day, most of them appealing to the flesh. Magazine ads, even in Christian magazines, are so sophisticated that trying to attend to the article beside the ad is like trying to do algebra homework in Times Square on New Year's Eve.[2] Only daily reflection and occasional longer periods of sustained contemplation can equip us to be more than survivors in a secular or neopagan society. But reflection does not come easily to us.

For many people silence is violence. They step into their cars and flick on the radio or put in a cassette. They are uncomfortable during a period of silence in worship and so must fill up every moment with religious chatter. If they were silent they would be forced to come to themselves like the prodigal in the far country, to confront their false selves and to let God give them new selves.

Solitude: Planned Availability

In Chaim Potok's novel *The Chosen*, the son of a Hasidic rabbi and spiritual leader, a tzaddik, reflects on his upbringing in which his father never spoke to him except over Torah, the Scriptures.

> My father himself never talked to me, except when we studied together. He taught me with silence. He taught me to look into myself, to find my own strength, to walk around inside myself in company with my soul. When his people would ask him why he was so silent with his son, he would say to them that he would not like to talk, words are cruel, words play tricks, they distort what is in the heart, they conceal the heart, the heart speaks through silence. One learns of the pain of others by suffering one's own pain, he would say, by turning inside oneself, by finding one's own soul. . . . For years his silence bewildered and frightened me, though I always trusted him, I never hated him. And when I was old enough to understand, he told me that of all people a tzaddik especially must know of pain.[3]

But silence does not guarantee solitude. And solitude is not the same thing as loneliness.

When we are *lonely* we reach out to other people to fill the void of our lives, and we cling to them to meet needs in ourselves. If there are not people willing to do this for us, we may escape into busyness to avoid the further conversion of our own souls. *Solitude*, in contrast, is different from loneliness. It is intentional isolation from others and planned availability to God.[4] It is what Jesus sought when he sent the crowd away. Loneliness may serve a spiritual purpose; it can propel us into the world of faith. It can also, as William Collins says in "A Sermon from Hell," "encapsulate us in a pathological cocoon of self-pity and self-imposed isolation."[5] When we are lonely we know we are alone. Solitude, in contrast, is the experience of silence in which we discover we are not alone. Loneliness is usually involuntary. But solitude is the grace of turning involuntary loneliness into a reaffirmation that we are in the presence of God and positioned to experience his friendship. In solitude we are least alone. So, as William Collins says, while "loneliness may be experienced as abandonment, solitude is experienced as dialogue,"[6] even if it is dialogue with God about his absence, as it was for the Psalmist (Ps. 22).

Thanksgiving: Waging War on Discontentment

The first movement of the soul toward God when we are alone should be gratitude. It was for lack of gratitude and reverence that the Gentiles who "although they knew God . . . neither glorified him as God nor gave thanks to him" (Rom. 1:21), were given over (1:24, 26, 28) to experience what we call sins, but in reality were symptoms of the fundamental sin of ingratitude. The original sin from the Garden onward has been to turn away from simple love for God and to cease practicing continuous thanksgiving in the midst of ordinary life. John Calvin said, "We are surrounded by God's benefits. The best use of these benefits is an unceasing expression of gratitude."[7]

The three phrases in 1 Thessalonians 5:16-18 hang together like the angles of a triangle: rejoice always, pray constantly, give thanks in all circumstances. There is a similar emphasis in Paul's letter to the Philippians where Paul confesses that he has learned the secret of being content in any and all circumstances (Phil. 4:4-12). When I first read this passage I said to myself, I have learned the secret of being *dis*content in almost every circumstance of my life! So I am learning from Philippians the secret of waging war on discontentment: thanksgiving—making our requests known with a grateful heart. Being content has almost nothing to do with the circumstances of our lives and almost everything to do with whether we refer everything to God in humble gratitude. There is nowhere else we can serve the Lord than where we are right now. Oswald Chambers put this in his deeply direct way: "Never allow the thought—'I can be of no use where I am'; because you certainly can be of no use where you are not."[8]

The older son in the parable of the two prodigals (Luke 15:11-32) was positioned circumstantially to receive all the remaining inheritance and to enjoy the Father's presence daily, but he felt cheated. "You never gave me . . ." (Luke 15:29) was the attitude of his heart, while in reality the father could say, "Everything I have is yours" (15:31). Gratitude had not broken his stony heart when the curtain came down on the drama. Yet the younger son came home penniless, with the slim hope of getting a job, and was surprised by joy. While his body was in the far country, his heart turned toward home and the waiting father. The older son's body was at home, but it seems his heart was in the far country secretly desiring the interesting sins of his brother's escapades. While still reflecting on the parable we can explore another discipline of the journey upward.

Confession: Being Honest with God

We cannot be positive all the time any more than we can breathe *out* all the time. Sometimes in the Psalms a person does *not* start with gratitude, but rather with a lament. Gratitude often comes later, when the person has "told it like it is." Sometimes gratitude can only be experienced when one has told the whole truth to God in confession.

Gratitude and confession are like the exhale and inhale of breathing. They belong together. Self-discovery apart from God-discovery leads to dangerous egoism. Sometimes this egoism takes a disguised form of self-crucifixion or putting ourselves down emotionally as a way of ingratiating ourselves to God. In this case the cloak of pride is turned inside out, but it is still pride because "I" is still in the center. No one is saved by either positive or negative works. Even a negative self-image does not commend us to God's favor.

So to tell the whole truth about ourselves to God is a miracle. To be completely candid, hiding neither behind a mask of presumed goodness, or in a cloud of self-loathing, to admit our nature just as it is now, without excusing, justifying, or pretending, to claim to be neither less nor more than we are, to be able to say, "My name is Jacob" is an idle dream apart from grace. It might even be dangerous. God deliberately clothes the hiding and naked Adam until he is ready to be shamelessly naked again (Gen. 3:21).

Blaise Pascal captured this so well in his *Pensées*. "The man who knows God but does not know his own misery, becomes proud. The man who knows his own misery but does not know God, ends in despair. The incarnation shows man the greatness of his own misery by the greatness of the remedy which he acquired."[9]

Authenticity comes not by introspection but by yielding ourselves just as we are to the loving God who wishes to reside in us. In the presence of the God of Jacob, who is also the God and Father of Jesus, we can afford to be honest. We cannot afford to be dishonest, because God can bless only real people, not casted characters.

Start with the Ten Commandments (Exod. 20:1-17). Walk through each commandment slowly and leisurely and ask God to reveal to you what you must see in the light of his presence. For example, when you read the first commandment—*Thou shalt have none other Gods but me*—ask yourself questions like these: Who comes first in my life—God or myself? His will or mine? Have I been vain or boastful about my looks, clothing, ability, possessions, family background, success? Belittled others for their sins, poverty, race or religion? Have I been sorry for myself, or stubborn, bossy, or dictatorial? Refused to apologize, admit myself wrong? Have I learned true humility?[10]

As an alternative one might work through the fruits of the Spirit (Gal. 5:22-23): love, joy, peace, patience, kindness, goodness, faithfulness, gentleness and self-control. Ponder each fruit and consider how this fruit was manifested in Christ's life. Then ask whether there is evidence of the Christ-life in you. These fruits are not something *we* can accomplish, and they cannot be obtained quickly. They are the fruits of the Spirit, not the vegetables of the Spirit. But the recognition of a need and failure is an implicit prayer that Christ might dwell in you more deeply.

Repentance, says C. S. Lewis, "is not something God demands of you before He will take you back and which He could let you off if you chose; it is simply a description of what going back is like."[11] The returning prodigal gives us some important clues:

After he had spent everything (Luke 15:14): A sense of need is a God-given thing. Thank God for the experience of disillusionment, for everything which drives us to him.

He came to his senses (15:17): One indication that he has come to his senses is that while he began by saying "father give me," he now requests "father make me." He wants to be made something he cannot make himself. This is a sure sign of sober thinking.

He planned—I will go to my father (15:18): He rehearsed his confession.

He put feet to his thoughts (15:20): He got up and went to his father.

Take Luke 15:11-32 as a guideline, and make the journeys of the two prodigals a structure for your own journey upward using the following questions: Where are you now in life? In the far country? At home, but not really at home? What problems or needs are reminding you that your true home is in God? What fears do you have as you make your way closer to God? Where do you need to be found by the seeking Father today? In what ways may you underestimate what God has in mind as you come to him? How has God surprised you already in your approaching him? What evidence do you have that he is seeking you even more than you are seeking him? What does the image of the celebration do to your conception of the Father's presence and home? How does your relationship with your brother or sister affect your experience of the Father? When, if ever, have you failed to enter God's rest because you have doubted the sincerity of your brother's or sister's conversion or felt that too much attention was being paid to him or her? Do you regard the Christian life in terms of performance (like the elder brother) or relationship (like the father)? How has the Father rewarded you? Do you think he has rewarded you sufficiently? Do you have anger against God? How does the Father show he loves you even when you are like the older brother?

Bible Meditation: Crawling through Scripture

Confession expresses the hunger of our hearts. God's Word feeds that hunger. The fourth-century father John Chrysostom is fearlessly direct in pressing the case for the spiritual reading of Scripture by the ordinary Christian. In this extended quotation Chrysostom deals with the unspoken thought of the layperson who feels he or she is too busy to attend to the Word of God and, in passing, shows that it was not any easier to follow Jesus in the ancient world:

> Your wife provokes you, for example, your son grieves you, your servant angers you, your enemy plots against

you, your friend envies you, your neighbor curses you, your fellow soldier trips you up, often a law suit threatens you, poverty troubles you, loss of your property gives you grief, prosperity puffs you up, misfortune depresses you, and many causes and compulsions to discouragement and grief, to conceit and desperation surround us on all sides, and a multitude of missiles falls from everywhere. Therefore we have a continuous need for the full armor of the Scriptures. . . . We must thoroughly quench the darts of the devil and beat them off by continual reading of the divine Scriptures. For it is not possible, not possible for anyone to be saved without continually taking advantage of spiritual reading.[12]

But how are we to read the Bible? Reading large passages of Scripture every day with a view to reading through the Bible each year is a wonderful discipline, and there is an excellent lectionary to assist you in this.[13] But on a day alone there is great gain in crawling through the Scripture, attending to each word and making it our own. The air is, in a sense, full of melodies—or more accurately, electromagnetic waves—that carry thousands of radio and television programs to us. But we must tune in to the one message we must hear and make our own. Bible meditation is more than, though not less than, exegesis, which is the science of understanding the text in its context.

Bible expositors are tempted to make biblical interpretation into a mere science, reducing the text to its structural units and analyzing the words, and investigating through hermeneutics both the writer's and the reader's motives and understandings. This exercise need not take away from the spiritual reading of the text and is an important function in gaining the plain sense of the text. But it may be a dangerous diversion from actually *hearing* the Word. Søren Kierkegaard compared the scholar consulting his commentaries with a small boy stuffing his britches with a pillow to cushion the licking he was about to get. As James Houston says, "The theoretical disputations on hermeneutics seem mostly to have little immediate application to the act of 'Bible reading.'"[14] Meditation on the text does not eliminate the need for sound exegesis, but it does take one beyond it through internalizing what one has read and heard so that our fundamental longings and addictions are addressed by the inseminating Word of God. What Houston wishes to recover is not merely the *lectio divina* of Medieval monasticism, but the experience of biblical meditation suggested by the Scripture itself. The words used in the Bible for "meditate" imply the use of both the mind and heart.

The Hebrew word *siach* means to muse, go over in one's mind, rehearse (Gen. 24:63; Ps. 119:15, 23, 27, 48, 78, 148). *Hagah* means to mutter or meditate. It is used of the sound characteristic of the moaning of the dove (Isa. 38:14), or the growling of the lion over its prey (Isa. 31:4). The righteous ponder or brood upon the proper answer (Prov. 15:28) and then talk about wisdom (Ps. 37:30) or God's righteousness (Ps. 35:28). *Promeleteo* in the New Testament means to meditate before what you shall answer or to practice a speech (Luke 21:14). In meditating we imbibe the Word (Rev. 10:10), chew on it as a cow chews its cud, make it our very own. It is a prayerful way of reading the Bible.

One way to make a beginning is to take an incident in the Gospels (such as John 5:1-15 or John 21:1-19) and put yourself into the story. Linger long enough on each detail of the story until you have re-created the whole drama. Allow yourself prayerfully to identify with more than one character in the drama, and allow Jesus to minister to you as he ministers to the people in the story. Ignatian Exercises make use of this means of Bible meditation, and some modern interpreters have made excellent adaptions of these.[15]

A psalm can be made into a personal song. Psalm 116 says "I love the Lord, for he heard my voice; he heard my cry for mercy. . . . For you, O Lord, have delivered my soul from death, my eyes from tears, my feet from stumbling, that I may walk before the Lord in the land of the living." Put your own story in the three occasions for gratitude: deliverance from the death of my soul, deliverance from the burden of despair, and deliverance from moral failure. Or take Psalm 77, where the psalmist meditates on his complaint (verse 3), on his experience of the absence of God (verse 6), and on the works of God (verse 12) and thereby turns his experience of the absence of God into a meditation on the deeds of God.[16] This is a good example of turning the experience of loneliness and abandonment into the opportunity to experience dialogue in solitude.

We are inundated with information today, even information about God, but there is a famine today of *hearing* the Word of God. Smugness about the all-sufficiency of an initial conversion has made our hearts lazy. Pascal once said that we would not be seeking God if we had not already found him. But the converse is equally true: If we are not still seeking him, it is doubtful that we have found him. This is, as Tozer says, the soul's paradox of love. He puts it this way:

> Everything is made to center upon the initial act of "accepting Christ" (a term, incidentally, which is not found in the Bible) and we are not expected thereafter to crave any further revelation of God to our souls. We have been snared in the coils of a spurious logic which insists that if we have found Him we need no more seek Him.[17]

The hungry heart will hunger even more.

On one hand, these three chapters on the day alone appear to be an invitation to hard work. Solitude does not come easily to our Walkman-inundated culture. And spiritual disciplines like the ones we have already explored are hard work in just the same way as cultivating the soil, planting the seed, watering and fertilizing it, and waiting is hard work for the farmer. But, on the other hand, the seed grows by itself.

Spiritual disciplines, properly understood, are not attempts to reach a distant and elusive God, but ways of removing obstacles and creating new channels of response to the seeking Father. God does the finding, and our seeking is—even from the first movement within our souls—an active response to his finding us. So disciplines are not the means of gaining godliness; they are the fruit of godliness.

14
The Journey Inward

"It is easier to sail many thousands of miles through cold and storm and cannibals in a government ship, with five hundred men and boys to assist one than it is to explore the private sea, the Atlantic and Pacific Ocean of one's being alone."
—Henry David Thoreau

"As I see it, we shall never succeed in knowing ourselves unless we seek to know God."—St. Teresa

Jung tells the story of a clergyperson who had been working fourteen hours a day and was suffering from emotional exhaustion. Jung advised that he should work eight hours a day, then go home and spend the evening alone in his study. The clergyperson agreed to follow Jung's advice precisely. He worked eight hours and then went home to his study, where he played some Chopin and read a novel by Hesse. The following day he read Thomas Mann and played Mozart. On the third day he went to see Jung and complained that he was no better. "But you didn't understand," Jung replied, on hearing his account. "I didn't want you with Herman Hesse or Thomas Mann or even Mozart or Chopin. I wanted you alone with yourself."

"Oh, but I can't think of any worse company," answered the clergyman.

Jung replied, "And yet this is the self you inflict on other people fourteen hours a day."[1]

The extent to which people will go to avoid self-confrontation is awesome. Work and leisure are the most common dodges. But by far the most dangerous are the diversions created when religion itself is used to escape the discovery of who I am. Service to God and theologizing easily become a way of hiding like Adam among the trees of the garden escaping from the voice and presence of the Lord God. Some ministering people have what Eric Fromm called "market-oriented personalities" who sell themselves to be or do whatever procures them signs of acceptance, so delaying the needed journey within. Fortunately our God is more willing to seek than we are to be found.

Hide and Be Found

As a little child I loved to play "hide and seek" in the back lanes and yards of our neighborhood in Toronto. For a child, play is work, and therefore the meaning we adults attach to work is frequently applied to a child in his or her play. For me, as I now look back, it was more than a game. I dreaded being "it" because the person who was "it" had to stand at a lamp-post and count to a hundred with his eyes closed while all the others ran into hiding. Some of my friends were very clever in the way they hid themselves, in closets, shrubs, cars, and sometimes high overhead on the roofs of our backyard garages. The first person to be caught had to be "it" next time and find everyone else. I am not a very patient seeker and I was always glad when someone else got caught first and so became "it."

But I also did not want to be "lost" for very long, unlike some of the my street friends who would take fiendish delight in locating themselves in some nook that virtually no one could find. At the end of the game, occasionally, one of my friends would come reluctantly out of hiding, having missed a turn or so. The others had given up on him! He either had to remain lost forever or give himself up. I found myself in the tension of not being a patient seeker but also not wanting to be lost. In hindsight I think I was more of a seeker than a hider. But more than being a seeker I strangely *wanted to be found*, which is not what the game was supposed to be about. This child's work was an unintended preparation for my journey of faith.

Often I did not hide myself very well so that I would be found. But at the same time, I did not want to be caught too quickly and so to have the responsibility for finding everyone else. The secret of playing this game—which is child's work and a parable of our spiritual journey—is to hide oneself with a view to being found at the right time and in the right way. Otherwise one would come to the end of the game and reluctantly, with considerable embarrassment rather than victory, be forced to reveal oneself as one who cannot and will not be found. So it is with God, who is "it" all the time and ever shall be.

So my deepest need is to be found. Like Jacob I have a God who is longing to bless me if only I will be real and tell him the whole truth about myself. Jacob spent twenty years avoiding himself until his tryst with the Angel-man and his final struggle with God. "What is your name?" (Gen. 32:27) is the question with which God had been seeking him for all those years of self-evasion. God had confronted him over and again with the invitation to be real. So Jacob's external journey from place to place (from Beersheba to Bethel, to Haran, to Jabbok, to Shechem, to Bethel) is the exteriorization of an inner journey that was equally significant, a journey of self-discovery in the presence of the seeking Father. It is a journey positively called forth by ministry, whether in the marketplace or the church.

Ministry and Spirituality

Ministry and spirituality are interdependent; each feeds the other. On the one hand, we minister most authentically from what we experience God actually doing in our lives; truth is strained through our personality. On the other hand, the experience of reaching out in ministry raises questions about ourselves that call forth the need to be found during a day alone, questions such as these:

Why am I so sensitive to criticism?
Why am I driven to fill in all the gaps in my datebook?
Why do I find it hard to give up places and positions?
Why do I often put myself down in front of others?
Why am I so competitive?
Why is it so important to succeed?
Why am I unable to let go of the pain of others?
Why do I need people so desperately, and why am I so
  afraid to be alone?
Why am I discontent?
Why do certain kinds of people get under my skin?
Why do I tend to burn out relationships?
Why am I so busy?
Why am I so unmotivated?

These and a host of questions like them surface in the rough-and-tumble of everyday ministry. But there are greater reasons to embark on the journey inward than simple need.

Theology of Self-Discovery

Christian experience is transformational. It took only a few hours to get the prodigal out of the far country, but undoubtedly it took many years to get the far country out of the prodigal. He was instantly forgiven and justified, declared to be not guilty and given the tokens of acceptance: the ring, the robe, and the reception. But there were habitual thoughts to conquer, attacks of guilt for wasting the inheritance, and the lingering censure of his brother. So salvation in Christ is both immediate and progressive. It only takes a microsecond for faith to break into our souls and to know that Jesus has done enough on the cross to make it possible for us to come to God just as we are, without one plea, except that Christ's blood was shed for us. But working out that salvation takes time (Phil. 2:12).

The Christian person is a person undergoing reconquest. While there has been a change of government from the revolutionary to the constitutional (to the Lord), there are pockets of resistance and a fleshly predisposition to be dealt with by daily crucifixion and daily aspiration of the Spirit. It is not as simple as saying that our spirits are saved, but our souls and bodies need to begin to experience the full impact of our new spiritual life. In fact human persons, biblically understood, are not three-compartment beings (spirit-soul-body) but personal wholes. We do not *have* spirits; we *are* spirits. We do not *have* souls (the emotional and intellectual dimensions of our personhood); we *are* souls. We do not *have* bodies (as if they were merely the shells of the inner life); we *are* bodies. So to be touched at any dimension of our personhood is to be touched as a whole person. Herein lies the strong biblical prohibition against sexual sin because it joins *the spirit* with unsuitable partners (1 Cor. 6:15-17). While salvation can touch us initially at any point: body, soul, or spirit, the whole will be affected, though not immediately. And the full reconquest and healing of the whole person is *never* accomplished by that first touch, as eternally significant as that touch is.

So we are engaged in a process. The prolonged time of the process is part of God's gift. If we were instantly justified, healed, emotionally transformed, and totally integrated in one mighty miracle, we might not learn to love God or know ourselves as we will through the upward, inner, and outward journeys. E. Stanley Jones says this magnificently:

> Conversion is a gift and an achievement. It is an act of a moment and the work of a lifetime. You cannot achieve salvation by disciplines—it is the gift of God.
>
> But you cannot retain it without disciplines. If you try to attain salvation by disciplines you will be trying to discipline an unsurrendered self. You are sitting on the lid. The result will be tenseness instead of trust. . . . While salvation cannot be attained by discipline around an unsurrendered self, nevertheless when the self is surrendered to Christ and a new center formed, then you can discipline your life around that new center—Christ. Discipline is the fruit of conversion—not the root.[2]

In describing his life in one of his ashrams in India, E. Stanley Jones notes how they gave their servants one day off each week and volunteered to do the most menial jobs themselves, including cleaning the latrines, a job which normally only an outcast would touch. One day Jones asked a Brahmin convert to volunteer for this job. He shook his head slowly and said, "Brother Stanley, I'm converted, but I'm not converted that far."[3]

Incarnational Ministry

There are also ministry reasons for a day alone. Impersonal Christian ministry is unthinkable. All authentic ministry is incarnational; it comes through life to life, truth strained through personality. As images of Christ we are icons, incarnational signs that Jesus lives in this real world through real people. Changing the metaphor, we could speak of ourselves as Kodachrome transparencies that reveal almost nothing when one looks *at* them. But if you hold a transparency to the light and invite people to look at the light through it, a beautiful image can be seen. Old covenant thinking suggests that if we hide ourselves Christ will be most fully revealed. But under the new covenant we "with unveiled faces all reflect the Lord's glory, (and) are being transformed into his likeness with ever-increasing glory, which comes from the Lord, who is the Spirit" (2 Cor. 3:18).

Paul clearly emphasized that our experience of struggle in the Christian life is *itself* the arena of revelation of the living Christ for both ourselves and others. The molten gold of this gospel treasure flows through the cracks in personal earthenware vessels (2 Cor. 4:7). Orthodoxy in Christian experience according to Paul is being weak, knowing God is strong, and living the Cross-life at the intersection of our weakness and God's strength. If we try to find power in ministry in our personality, giftedness, background, and training, we exclude the authentic power of God, which can only come where there is acknowledged weakness (2 Cor. 13:4). My burden carries me daily to Jesus, who transforms my burden daily into a sacrament of Christ's power and grace made perfect through weakness.

What makes people "findable" is precisely what makes Christianity so odious to some. It is not the self-sufficient who are found by God, but those who embrace their own weakness, who would rather limp their way into the Promised Land, like Jacob, with a song of praise on their lips than to stride faultlessly in their own confidence. Christianity *is* a crutch. That is its greatness. Christ must be leaned upon to be known. Our burden carries us. God's grace can only be known by those who will admit they are creatures and not gods, creatures whose desperate hiding from God means that they now have only a weak and broken humanity to offer back to their Creator. To these God speaks triumphantly in Christ: "My grace is sufficient for you, for my power is made perfect in weakness" (2 Cor. 12:9). God's first words in Genesis to the hiding couple were "Where are you?" (Gen. 3:9); Christ's last words in the Gospel were "I am with you alway" (Matt. 28:20). Between the question and the affirmation we live by faith as found people. God will have it no other way. It has never been otherwise for the true saint. We have a God who insists that we be real.

15

Becoming Real

"Let him who cannot be alone beware of community. Let him who is not in community beware of being alone." —Dietrich Bonhoeffer

The number-one unforgivable sin in Western society is phoneyness. There is biblical reason for agreeing with this secular judgment. As Jacob found, God can only bless real people. So in this chapter we will consider three strategies for using a day alone in order to become more real.

Journal-Keeping

A discipline that encourages inner authenticity is keeping a journal. Psalm 42:5 is really a journal entry. In it David is talking to God in writing about his depression in the light of something greater than his own experience. "Why are you downcast, O my soul? Why so disturbed within me? Put your hope in God, for I will yet praise him, my Savior and my God." The Psalms are an eloquent witness that outpourings of emotions, hurts, fears, and resentments to God in prayer are not merely permitted; they are positively encouraged. One way of recognizing the Word of God in the Psalms is not merely to analyze the words of the Psalms, but rather to allow the God of the psalmist to be revealed through the quality of the psalmist's prayers. This is the metacommunication of the Psalms that turns out to be more important than the messages communicated within the Psalms. The

God revealed to us in the Psalms is One to whom we can bring the whole range of our experience, past and present, letting it pour right out just as it is. God is the only being in the whole universe who can "take" everything that is going on inside us. He encourages, through the Psalter, the struggling believer to express to God even hostility and anger toward God. The cross of Jesus is the full and final reception of his human hostility and God's final solution for it. If we had nothing but the Psalms to know God, we would conclude that God is interested in healing our feelings (6:6-9), our experiences of rejection (31:11-13; 137:8-9), our discouragements (142:3-4), our doubts (3:2), our unresolved problems, our hurts (6:2), and our guilt (103:3; 51:1-6).

So keeping a journal is like writing a letter to God, or writing out our prayers, or speaking to our own soul in the presence of Someone greater than our own experience. Then our absence of experience of God, or even our experience of the absence of God, can become a cry for more reality with God. It is essential that we let our thoughts and feelings flow out without editing and self-criticism, for we have a God to whom we can pour out the darkest and deepest things within us.

Madeleine L'Engle captures this astonishing accessibility of God to our inner life in this shockingly authentic poem:

I hate you, God.
Love, Madeleine.
                    I write my message on water
                    and at bedtime I tiptoe upstairs
                    and let it flow under your door.
When I am angry with you
I know that you are there
even if you do not answer my knock
even when your butler opens the door an inch
and flaps his thousand wings in annoyance
at such untoward interruption

and says that the master is not at home.
        I love you, Madeleine.
        Hate, God.
(This is how I treat my friends, he said to one great saint.
No wonder you have so few of them, Lord, she replied.)
        I cannot turn the other cheek
        It takes all the strength I have
        to keep my fist from hitting back
        the soldiers shot her baby
        the little boys trample the old woman
        the gutters are filled with groans
        while pleasure seekers knock each other down
        in order to get their tickets stamped first.
I'm turning in my ticket
and my letter of introduction.
You're supposed to do the knocking. Why do you burst
my heart?
        How can I write you
        to tell you that I'm angry
        when I've been given the wrong address
        and I don't even know your real name?
I take hammer and nails
and tack my message on two crossed pieces of wood:
        Dear God
        is it too much to ask you
        to bother to be?
        Just show your hindquarters
        and let me hear you roar.
Love,
Madeleine.[1]

One temptation in keeping a journal, whether daily or weekly, is to bring a utilitarian focus to the discipline. The discipline must work. It must be effective. It must bring results in terms of a deeper life in God. In reality the best way to have spiritual experiences is not to seek them, but

merely to seek the Lord. Journal-keeping is a special temptation to the Christian whose ministry is public communication. As we write we might even begin to think, *This would
make a great sermon* or *I can use this with my adult class*, which
destroys its fundamental purpose: to tell the whole truth to
God for God's sake. Some experiences recorded in a journal
can be shared in due course, but the market-oriented personality will always be looking for something to "sell" even
in the personal journal and so lose its contemplative benefit.
Meditation has been defined as turning from the things of
this world to the things of God, while contemplation,
defined in this light, is turning our attention from the
"things" of God to attend to God himself—a much more
important discipline. Even the journey inward may be contemplative in this sense: The discovery of ourselves is *for*
God and *in* God. Walter of Hilton, a fourteenth-century
pioneer in the spiritual life, wrote the following words:

> First, you ought to love yourself only in God, or else for
> the sake of God. You are loving yourself in God when your
> life is rightly ordained in grace and virtues. You are not
> loving your own self, but that righteousness and virtue
> which God gives you. You are loving yourself *in* God, for
> actually you are not loving your own self but rather God.
> Moreover, you are to love yourself for God's sake, and
> inasmuch as you are in deadly sin and want to be made
> righteous and virtuous before him, you are not loving
> yourself as you are (which is unrighteous), but actually as
> you would be. Just so should you love your fellow Chris-
> tians.[2]

Such divinely-inspired and divinely-directed self-love
usually does not come merely from writing a journal if there
are profoundly influential scars from our childhood that
influence our adult life. So we must explore another way to
spend a day alone.

Walking through your Life with Jesus

For many Christians the past is not in the past, except in the ultimate sense of being justified by faith. But in the day-to-day interchanges they are living out past hurts today, reacting in the light of unforgiven hurts against them, and repeating patterns that may have been handed down through many generations. Especially if we were rejected at birth, or our parents wished we were another sex, or our parents had attempted to abort us, or we were sexually or physically abused, or we witnessed a profoundly hurtful trauma, or we were profoundly hurt in romantic relationships from which we have never recovered, or were scarred by failure at school, in the neighborhood, in the marketplace, or in church ministry, we may be in need of soul-healing, or the healing of memories as it is sometimes called.

Profoundly painful events in our past may have been suppressed merely to achieve survival, but they continue to affect us when we are touched by the opposite sex, or when a contemporary situation triggers some of the old feelings. Sometimes the violent anger that spills over, completely out of proportion to the triggering event, is a sign that there is an unhealed scar. Many Christian workers actually minister from this "hurt edge" and play the martyr, or evoke pity as a way of gaining control of situations and people. True joy in the Spirit is lacking because joy is the overflow of the Spirit in all dimensions of our personhood and when our whole personal history has been redeemed.

So it is a good thing to engage in the discipline of walking through your life with Jesus, asking him to show you the happy as well as sad events and relationships that comprise your personal story. Usually this takes several hours and may be done best in a retreat setting, because it takes action-oriented people several hours to stop long enough to get in touch with their own feelings. The theological reality behind this discipline is the statement of God to Jacob, and Jesus to us: "I am with you" (Gen. 28:15; 31:3). God is personally present through our entire lives from conception onward, even before we first felt the warmth of his love. God is unconditionally present and does not require either we ourselves or the other players in our life to be worthy of his presence. God is omnipotently present, for there is no experience we have had, no matter how painful or violent, that he cannot transform into an asset by his omnipotent grace. One reason why we so rarely experience full release and recovery of our past is that we are too theoretical and not specific enough in our desire to become whole. Our imagination can serve us in this.

Imagination is a good gift of God. By allowing ourselves to "hear, see, and feel" a past event through Spirit-inspired imagination we expound the experience, or relive it. The brain is like a video recorder and can, by the Spirit's prompting, recall everything, even experiences formerly too painful to be brought to light. But it is safe to go anywhere in our life with Jesus. And in walking through our life with Jesus we can safely ask him to show us pleasant and painful experiences that in his view are important for us to understand and express faith toward. It does not matter whether we start at the earliest memory of our infancy and work through our lives chronologically, or to start with the present and work backward.

As we encounter memories of experiences that are pleasant we can immediately thank Jesus for them. And as we encounter situations where we were hurt by others, we can prayerfully ask Jesus to show us his presence there, revealing his lordship and showing us what he will now do to that experience in the light of his victory on the cross. Far from leaving ourselves open to demons who come to us in the name of Jesus, this is a genuine act of worship to Jesus, provided that we do not reduce God to the picture we have of him, for this would be idolatry. The role of imagination in healing has been brilliantly expounded by Leanne Payne in

The Healing Presence. Usually we encounter one or two very painful experiences that are determinative of our present life. For example, in my own inner journey I have encountered time and again the hurt of not being affirmed, and it has been crucial for me to visualize the specific ways that Jesus more than makes up for this lack of affirmation in my childhood and youth. Where we have been profoundly sinned against, we can ask for grace to get to the point where we can say of those who have wounded us, "I forgive them, for they did not know what they were doing." Sometimes with very painful events, such as the discovery of the sources of homosexual tendencies, or the experience of sexual abuse, it is important to share this journey with at least one other experienced prayer counselor. Often hours of prayer and counseling become intertwined before there is complete and substantial healing of profound hurt.

Until the resurrection of the body, there is no complete and final healing in this life. Even the resurrected body of Jesus, as revealed to the first disciples, bore scars on the hands and the side. But these scars were gloriously transformed. What once were marks of sin had now become the means of faith for people like Thomas who were invited to touch and to believe. So too the scars of our past will not be eliminated by this discipline. But they can be transformed to become the means of unceasing gratitude to God in our own hearts and the means of faith for others. Perhaps in heaven these scars will still exist, and may be part of our corporate unceasing praise of the Lamb and part of the beauty of the new heaven and the new earth.

Befriending Nature

One way of practicing the presence of Jesus in a rural context, or as part of a prayer retreat, is to befriend nature. The outer world of God's creation can minister to the interior life by evoking corresponding images and realities. Once on a retreat we were invited to go for a walk and ask God to show us something in nature that suggested something about ourselves that God wanted us to realize. As I walked through snow-covered fields I encountered a strong, tall, stately hemlock in its transcendent majesty. That, I thought, is not me. Nor did I find myself in a small bush of young trees bent over by the weight of the fresh snow. I encountered a huge rotting stump of a tree that had once been. Not that, either. But then I discovered a tree that had once been used as a fence-post. The farmer had wrapped the barb wire around the post and secured his fence with the tree. The tree could grow around the wire but could not remove it. As the tree continued to grow it was progressively throttled by the wire noose. But apparently, one day the wire had been cut off. The tree was released to grow freely and well, which it did. But the scar was there—not now the scar of a throttling vice or hurt, but the witness that this is a tree that has now been freed. "That," I said in the Spirit, "is me."

This glorious inner transformation of becoming real takes time, as the following quotation suggests. In the children's story *The Velveteen Rabbit* by Margery Williams, two nursery animals are engaged in conversation about the theme of this chapter:

> The skin horse had lived longer in the nursery than any of the others. He was so old that his brown coat was bald in patches and showed the seams underneath, and most of the hairs in his tail had been pulled out to string bead necklaces. He was wise, for he had seen a long succession of mechanical toys arrive to boast and swagger, and by-and-by break their mainsprings and pass away, and he knew that they were only toys, and would never turn into anything else. For nursery magic is very strange and wonderful, and only those play-things that are old and wise and experienced like the Skin Horse understand all about it.

"What is *real?*" asked the Rabbit one day, when they were lying side by side near the nursery fender, before Nana came to tidy the room. "Does it mean having things that buzz inside you and a stick-out handle?"

"Real isn't how you are made," said the Skin Horse. "It's a thing that happens to you. When a child loves you for a long, long time, not just to play with, but *really* loves you, then you become Real."

"Does it hurt?" asked the Rabbit.

"Sometimes," said the Skin Horse, for he was always truthful. "When you are Real you don't mind being hurt."

"Does it happen all at once, like being wound up," he asked, "or bit by bit?"

"It doesn't happen all at once," said the Skin Horse. "You become. It takes a long time. That's why it doesn't often happen to people who break easily, or have sharp edges, or who have to be carefully kept. Generally, by the time you are Real, most of your hair has been loved off, and your eyes drop out and you get loose in the joints and very shabby. But these things don't matter at all, because once you are Real you can't be ugly, except to people who don't understand."

"I suppose *you* are Real?" said the Rabbit. And then he wished he had not said it, for he thought the Skin Horse might be sensitive. But the Skin Horse only smiled.

"The Boy's Uncle made me Real," he said. "That was a great many years ago; but once you are Real you can't become unreal again. It lasts for always."[3]

PART SIX

A DAY WITH NEIGHBORS

16
The Poor

"There was once a wild goose who went to live with some tame geese. He was committed to liberate them from their mediocre lives. The wild goose lived with the tame geese for a year, and he enjoyed the rich food, comfortable shelter and easy life. Each year, when the wild geese flew overhead, he would flutter his wings, prepare to join them but settle down again in the farmyard. Ten years passed and the wild goose became tame, and it forgot how to fly." —Søren Kierkegaard

"When you give a luncheon or dinner, do not invite your friends, your brothers or relatives, or your rich neighbors; if you do, they may invite you back and so you will be repaid. But when you give a banquet, invite the poor, the crippled, the lame, the blind, and you will be blessed. Although they cannot repay you, you will be repaid at the resurrection of the righteous." —Jesus, Luke 14:12-14

Though my parents never intended it, their spiritual nurturing included exposing me to the ministry of the poor to the rich. They built our family home on a three-acre plot next door to a one room shack without water, electricity, indoor plumbing, or a furnace. Albert Jupp lived with his aged and ill mother in that smelly, dank shack. As he was occupied with the care of his mother, Albert was unable to hold down a steady job. Somehow they eked out an existence beside the Stevens, their rich next-door neighbors. Today the rich hardly see the poor except on television or from an air-conditioned tour bus.

159

Each night Albert would get a pail of water at our outside tap, which was always kept running, even in the dead of winter, when our neighbors had their taps safely protected from freezing. My mother was one of the most generous souls on earth, and her sensitive conscience would not allow her to set a fine meal before our family without thinking of Albert and his mother. So night after night I was asked to make a pilgrimage up the hill to the shack with two portions from our table for our poor neighbors. I confess that as a teenager I usually resented doing this. But what I think was bothering me was how that nightly visit to the Jupps made me think about my own existence as a rich young man. Daily I was confronted existentially with the truth that the rich cannot know God well without relating to the poor.

The Proximity of the Poor

Since those early days in Ontario the world has shrunk some more. Theoretically, loving my poor neighbor should be easier than ever now that television brings the specter of starving multitudes into my living room and makes media neighbors out of the Third World. In two days of jet travel my wife and I can relocate to a Kenyan village and be with our poor friends in Africa, whom we visit year after year. But being real neighbors to the poor seems harder than ever. Zoning bylaws in our modern cities institutionalize and separate the suburbs and the inner city. Today, Albert Jupp would not be allowed to live beside my family in our Vancouver home. The rich usually do not see the poor, let alone live near them. Physical proximity would help, but to be a neighbor to the poor we must bring the poor near in our hearts.

To expose this heart issue, Jesus told a parable that recapitulates my youthful experience: a rich man and a poor man named Lazarus, side by side confronting each other's existence on a daily basis (Luke 16:19-31).

As a master teacher Jesus uses an economy of illuminating details. The rich man feasted in luxury every day and was dressed in purple and fine linen. He had a mansion with a gate. The poor man was covered with sores, longed to eat the crumbs from the rich man's table, and was powerless even to get himself to the gate of the mansion, where he would beg day by day. With one final stroke Jesus completes the picture of an untouchable person: "Even the dogs came and licked his sores" (16:21). In this case proximity did not help the rich man befriend the poor, for Lazarus had become a fixture in the mansion, like the pictures of emaciated children in various magazines.

In the parable, the importance of the spiritual discipline which the poor become to the rich is underlined when the rich man and Lazarus both died. The rich man went to Hades, and the poor man went to the bosom of Abraham (Jewish heaven). Death changed everything, even the rich man's heart. In Hades the rich man repented and, in his moment of reversed fortune, wanted the poor man to minister to him by dipping his finger in cool water to cool his tongue in the flame. But it was too late. So he pleaded with Father Abraham to send Lazarus back from the dead to persuade his five brothers to abandon their loveless affluence lest they come to the same tragic end. It is common to spiritualize Luke's message of interracial and total salvation in Jesus and thereby miss the social justice that comes if not before death, then at least after (Luke 6:20-26).

The teaching of Jesus leaves us with the unmistakable challenge to have a hands-on relationship with the poor and to accept some form of voluntary impoverishment. We must do this for the sake of the poor and for the sake of our own souls. A newspaper article asks "Why should we care about the Third World?" and answers in this way: "Because our economic, environmental and political future is inextricably linked with it."[1] But there is a deeper reason. The rich cannot be saved without the poor. It is a matter of spirituality. Clark

Pinnock, a Canadian theologian says "A story like that of Dives and Lazarus ought to explode in our hands when we read it sitting in our well-covered tables while the third world stands outside."[2]

The Friendship of the Poor

There is no doubt in my mind that in telling two parables about money and friendship (the shrewd manager and the rich man and Lazarus—Luke 16), and by placing them in juxtaposition, Jesus and Luke intend to motivate us to make friends with the poor. With outrageous freedom Jesus tells about a shrewd manager (Luke 16:1-9) who used money to make friends by reducing the loans owed to his master so when he would lose his job these friends would look after him forever. The magnetic center of this parable is a shocking exhortation from the lips of Jesus: "I tell you, use worldly wealth to gain friends for yourselves, so that when it is gone, you will be welcomed into eternal dwellings" (16:9). The second parable, Lazarus and the rich man, is given as an empowering negative example of a person who did not use his wealth to make friends of the poor and thus was not welcomed by them into an eternal home. Sandwiched in between these two parables is the word about the Law and the Prophets (16:16-18), which uniformly teach mercy to the poor.

The thrust of Luke 16 is the call to use our money to make friends with the poor, the sick, the powerless, the stranger, and the refugee. The unconverted heart believes that there is nothing the poor can do for us. They will not advance our cause or increase our security. But these two parables make the daring claim that what we gain through befriending the poor is love. Often the poor are richer than the rich in the treasures that really matter—in relationships.

The Mask of the Poor

In a remarkable series of seven sermons on the parable of the rich man and Lazarus, the fourth-century church Father, John Chrysostom addressed the illusions of wealth. Poverty and wealth, he says, are only masks. Just as the person in the theater wearing a king's mask may in reality be a ropemaker or a coppersmith, "in the same way here, sitting in this world as if in a theater and looking at the players on the stage, when you see many rich people, do not think they are truly rich, but that they are wearing the masks of rich people. . . . If you take off his mask, open up his conscience, and enter into his mind, you will often find there a great poverty of virtue."[3] The rich have everything except the capacity to give, so they give crumbs from the table. In reality the rich are very poor, while the poor are rich in generosity. Eternity revealed the true poverty of the rich man: "So poor indeed that he was not master of even a drop of water, but had to beg for this and did not obtain it by begging."[4]

In these prophetic sermons, Chrysostom argues that the rich are not owners of their wealth but stewards for the poor.

> Just as an official in the imperial treasury, if he neglects to distribute where he is ordered, but spends instead for his own indolence, pays the penalty and is put to death, so also the rich man is a kind of steward of the money which is owed for the distribution to the poor. He is directed to distribute it to his fellow servants who are in want. So if he spends more on himself than his need requires, he will pay the harshest penalty hereafter.[5]

Appealing to the prophets of the Old Testament (Mal. 3:8-10) Chrysostom warns about the spiritual dangers of the rich. Failing to share with the poor will be counted as theft. The rich "hold the goods of the poor even if they have inherited them from their fathers or no matter how they gathered their wealth."[6] "The most pitiable person of all," he says, "is the one who lives in luxury and shares his goods with nobody."[7] In contrast, *"By nourishing Christ* in poverty here and laying up great profit hereafter we will be able to attain the good things which are to come."[8] In this last quotation Chrysostom hints that ministering to the poor simultaneously heals the hearts of the rich and nourishes Jesus himself.

The Christ of the Poor

In the parable of the rich man and Lazarus, Jesus identifies with the poor man. In speaking of his own resurrection, Jesus puts into the mouth of Abraham the surprising statement that if the five brothers of the rich man for whom the rich man now feels belated love, "do not listen to Moses and the Prophets, they will not be convinced even if someone rises from the dead" (Luke 16:31). Jesus considers that his own future resurrection will have no evidential value to people who are not obeying the word they already have, the word to show mercy to the poor. In this subtle way Jesus puts himself into the story. He is present at our gate, waiting in the powerless person to be loved and to love.

I agree with Mother Teresa that we minister to Jesus when we show love to the poor, the stranger, the powerless, and the sick. The words of Jesus are meant to be taken with utter seriousness: "I tell you the truth, whatever you did for one of the least of these brothers of mine, you did for me" (Matt. 25:40).[9] As mentioned above, the point of departure for me from the statement that Jesus comes to us in the disguise of the sick, the unlovely, and the poorest of the poor is simply the surprise factor. In Matt. 25:39 the righteous say, "When did we see you (the Son of Man) sick or in prison and go to visit you?" Similarly, the unrighteous protest that *if they had known they were ministering to Jesus* they would gladly have done it: "When did we see you hungry or thirsty or a stranger or needing clothes or sick or in prison, and did not help you?" (25:44). It is the uncalculating, spontaneous loving service to the poor *because they are poor* that is rewarded, rather than the calculating service that seeks favor with the Lord by loving the poor.

Most of the time we will not be aware that we are nourishing Christ. To insist on this would not be to walk by faith. But we can be aware that but for Christ's presence *in us* we would not be able to give the most precious gift we can give—ourselves—or receive from the poor the precious gift they may wish to give—themselves. So to be a neighbor to the poor the rich must admit they are poor. We cannot go into the world and make friends for eternity as patrons. Carl Jung once said that he admired Christians because they saw Christ in those who are hungry, naked, in the hospital, and in prison. But what he could not understand "was that they could not see Christ in their own poverty."[10] We, who are one of the five brothers of the rich man (Luke 16:28) may, like Lazarus,[11] in the poverty of our riches look to God and find ourselves welcomed by both God and our poor neighbor. The only treasure we can take from this life to the next is the relationships we have made through Jesus.

17
The Stranger

"Holy solitaries is a phrase no more consistent with the gospel than holy adulterers. The gospel of Christ knows of no religion, but social; no holiness but social holiness. 'Faith working by love' is the length and breadth and depth and height of Christian perfection." —John Wesley

"Do not forget to entertain strangers, for by so doing some people have entertained angels without knowing it." —Hebrews 13:2

One of my African students at Regent College moved into a housing complex in suburban Vancouver and recorded his experience of culture shock in moving to urban Canada. In his home country, Tanzania, when a family moves into an area it is big news. People visit them, and they are expected to visit their neighbors without any prior notice. As they walk to the open market, to their place of work, or to the community well, they invariably will meet people along the way and speak with them. "In this place," Justyn Aforo noted, "people have cars and they can even get into their cars without stepping out of the house. People know one another and recognize each other on the street by the cars they drive and the jobs they do." The Aforos were deeply lonely and felt unwelcome. But rather than yield to despair, Justyn and his wife decided to show hospitality to the people who should have been their hosts. Though they were busy, full-time students and parents, they reached out to welcome their neighbors by celebrating the birthdays of neighboring children, having coffee times with the mothers, sponsoring community dinners, and developing a prayer fellowship for the few believers they discovered in their complex. *Hospitality* in the Greek language literally means love for the stranger. But in this case the stranger did the loving. In line with this, Jesus, when asked to define *neighbor,* refused to indicate our minimum responsibility and invited his hearers to *become* neighbors (Luke 10:36).

The Inhospitable Crowd

Tragically, the stranger often turns out to be a member of our own church, a workmate on the job, a next-door neighbor, or even a member of our own family. So hospitality is not a leisure-time hobby or an avocational interest. It is part of our continuous ministry of living for God seven days a week. The stranger in our lives is an invitation to relate to God—a spiritual discipline. And responding to our neighbor in love is a ministry. Teachers can become hosts to their students, lawyers with their clients, doctors with their patients, pastors with their parishioners, parents with their children. The spiritual logic behind this continuous ministry of hospitality is simply that we have a welcoming God, and his children should reflect his character. Jesus pictures the father running down the dusty road to embrace the returning younger prodigal and sponsoring a gala homecoming party (Luke 15:11-32). In the same parable Jesus pictures the father going outside the church to welcome the pouting older brother who was scandalized by the attention given to his good-for-nothing brother (15:28). Even Pharisees and self-righteous church people need hospitality. But much that passes for hospitality misses the mark of a genuine welcome. "Make yourself at home," someone will say. "I want you to feel free." We have all known the experience of being guests of a "host" who required us to act and speak a certain way, or who made us feel that we were not accepted as we were. When this imperious hospitality is thrust upon us, we feel manipulated and controlled, and often prefer to be alone. To offer genuine hospitality the heart of the host must be transformed.

From Hostility to Hospitality

Henri Nouwen describes this heart transformation as the spiritual movement from hostility to hospitality. We could easily regard the stranger as an intrusion, as someone who makes a claim on us simply because he or she exists. We were taught as children not to speak with strangers, and so now in the presence of a stranger we have a choice to make—a choice that seems to run counter to the lessons of childhood. Strangers seem threatening because their behavior is unknown and unpredictable. We are in danger of losing complete control over the circumstances of our lives. But for a genuine welcome to be given, this hostility must be recognized and displaced by hospitality.

Nouwen notes that the German word for hospitality is *Gastfreundschaf,* which means friendship for the guest, while the Dutch word *gastvrijheid* means the freedom of the guest. Using these two words he suggests that "hospitality wants to offer friendship without binding the guest and freedom without leaving him alone."[1] The essence of being a host is to offer our full and real presence to people. His analysis is brilliant and worthy of extensive quotation.

> Hospitality, therefore, means primarily the creation of a free space where the stranger can enter and become a friend instead of an enemy. Hospitality is not to change people, but to offer them space where change can take place. It is not to bring men and women over to our side, but to offer freedom not disturbed by dividing lines. It is not to lead our neighbor into a corner where there are no alternatives left, but to open a wide spectrum of options for choice and commitment. . . . It is not an educated

intimidation with good books, good stories and good works, but the liberation of fearful hearts so that words can find roots and bear ample fruit. . . . The paradox of hospitality is that it wants to create emptiness, not a fearful emptiness, but a friendly emptiness where strangers can enter and discover themselves as created free; free to sing their own songs, speak their own languages, dance their own dances; free also to leave and follow their own vocations. Hospitality is not a subtle invitation to adopt the life style of the host, but the gift of a chance for the guest to find his own. [2]

Building on Nouwen's splendid exposition I offer two further movements implicit in becoming a hospitable person: relational creativity and applied grace.

Relational Creativity

Unfortunately the word *creative* has been exclusively associated with the artistic and the aesthetic. But hospitality involves the creativity of forming an environment and attending to relationships in such a way that people are prized and liberated. But the parallel with artistic creativity is worth exploring. The artist must "see" something in his or her mind's eye before pen and paint is put to canvas. And in shaping and coloring the artist is actually making something new out of something that exists with great respect for the medium. In the same way a godly administrator is creative in finding new ways to empower employees so their talents and capacities are released. A good doctor is creative in offering the patient dignity as a person and not merely as a body. Making an accurate diagnosis is a matter that is sometimes as much of an art as a science. Church leaders truly welcome members when they renounce "using" the members of the church as resources to accomplish their own vision and plans for the church, and seek instead to discover and release the ministry and mission of the members of the church. Equipping is all about this. Homemakers show hospitality by creating an environment in which those who enter feel comfortable, heard, and appreciated. Elaborate provisions of food and furniture might frustrate creating a deep welcome. Often the poor are better at creative hospitality than the rich.

To press the idea of creativity a little further, there is an apocryphal story about Michelangelo that is worth repeating. The great artist was pushing a large hunk of stone down the street toward his sculpting studio when a neighbor cried out, "Hey, what are you going to do with that old piece of stone?" Michelangelo replied, "There is an angel in there that wants to come out."[3] The host has the same creative approach to people: There is a beautiful person inside who wants to come out. Perhaps this is part of the meaning of "entertaining angels without knowing it" (Heb. 13:2). Hospitable relationships are created, not constructed. There must be respect for the potential within the guest. And to evoke that potential the host must be willing to receive as well as to give. Elizabeth O'Connor speaks of this mutual ministry in this way:

> As the artist discovers that there is a direct relationship between the inner and outer forms of material, so we discover that creativity in our inner lives has a direct relationship to creativity in the world. *We can never be in the world only as its benefactors.* This does not make for authentic relationship. All that we genuinely do is very personal and calls into being our own personality.[4]

It is because creativity is so related to beauty and play that the creative person is, on one hand, the antitype of the useful person. As with the other spiritual disciplines this movement to create free and friendly space for people "works" best when it isn't work—or when there is playfulness in our work. We will explore this more fully in the section on Sabbath. But for the moment suffice it to say that relational creativity involves simply *enjoying* people. Parents especially need to enjoy their children because our deep need in growing to maturity is not just to be loved, but to be enjoyed and liked. No one wants to be the object on a love-an-unlovely-person project. And *agape* love, properly understood, makes undeserved favor, into simple joy. This is what grace does. On this point the fourth-century teacher John Chrysostom was eloquent.

Applied Grace

In his seven expositions of the parable of the rich man and Lazarus, Chrysostom reflects on why the poor man, Lazarus, went to the bosom of Abraham when he died.

> Abraham was hospitable. The rich man sees Lazarus with Abraham, in order that Lazarus may convict him of inhospitality. For that patriarch hunted out those who were going past and brought them into his own house; but this rich man overlooked the one who was lying inside his gate. Although he had such a treasure and an aid to his salvation, he passed him by every day and did not use in his need the poor man's help. But the patriarch was not a man like this, but quite the opposite: sitting before his door he angled for all those who were going by. Just as a fisherman casting his net into the sea not only draws up fish but often draws up gold and pearls, so this patriarch, angling for men, once caught angels as well, and (the remarkable part) without knowing it. Paul in his amazement at this praises him and says, "Do not neglect to show hospitality to strangers, for thereby some have entertained angels unawares" (Heb 13:2).[5]

The passage to which Chrysostom alludes (Gen. 18:1-15) has become the subject of one of the finest pieces of Russian

Orthodox iconography. In Rublev's "The Holy Trinity" the three angels that visited Abraham in the guise of the three strangers are pictured as the Father, Son, and Holy Spirit. In welcoming the stranger Abraham experiences the welcome within God himself and is given a promise. There is a deep truth in this artistic contemplation on the Scripture: when we welcome strangers we are participating in the mutual welcoming of the Holy Trinity, who in Jesus invites us to experience the welcome within God himself. Jesus prayed to the Father on our behalf, "May they be *in us*" (John 17:21). That is the ultimate hospitality.

I think my poor African friends have taught me more about hospitality than any books I have read. In rural Kenya Gail and I met a Tharaka tribal couple who were engaged in an informal marriage ministry with their friends and neighbors. Each day they shared the best they had with us, special foods and eggs, which are treasured in rural Kenya. More important, they shared their hearts with us. We shared our lives with them, especially what we had learned from the Bible on Christian marriage. Living in a remote area about one hundred miles from the nearest improved road, they could scarcely imagine how we live in Canada. "Do you have a big shamba-farm in Vancouver?" they asked through an interpreter.

"No, our shamba is very small. Our house occupies almost all the land."

"Then how do you grow your own food?"

"We don't," Gail and I replied. "We have to buy our food at the market."

From this brief conversation they concluded that we were poor, since only the poor cannot provide for themselves. On the way home that night Paul and Marisa talked about the fact that they had twenty acres of land and we have only a small patch. When they met us the next morning they informed us that they had decided to give us one of their twenty acres, if there was some way we could use it. We were moved to tears. We returned to Canada wondering whether Christians here would give one-twentieth of their total assets to a visiting stranger. Perhaps this is one reason why Christianity is in decline in my own country, and, in contrast, a beneficent forest fire in Kenya. Where there is true hospitality, God the Father, the Son, and the Holy Spirit delight to dwell.

18
The Outsider

"The idea that the service to God should have only to do with a church altar, singing, reading, sacrifice, and the like is without doubt but the worst trick of the devil. How could the devil have led us more effectively astray than by the narrow conception that service to God takes place only in church and by works done therein. . . . The whole world could abound with services to the Lord, Gottesdienste—not only in churches but also in the home, kitchen, workshop, field."—Martin Luther

Elder Blumhard once said that every Christian needs two conversions: first conversion to Christ and then to the world.[1] The church is the one organization that exists for the non-member. This idea has become widely accepted since it was first expressed this way years ago by Archbishop William Temple. A day with a neighbor is part of the Christian vocation. *Neighbor* as defined by Jesus is not merely the one who is near you. *Neighbor* is what we become when we reach out to those we might not otherwise embrace (Luke 10:29-37). It is not just physical proximity but the proximity of the heart that makes an insider out of an outsider. What we must explore in this chapter is why Christians resist the blessing of relating to outsiders and prefer the comfort of the company of insiders. Further we will discover what reaching out means to our relationship with God. And no book in the Bible is more evocative on this subject than the Old Testament book of Jonah.

Reaching Good People

While Jonah appears in the Bible in the section called the Minor Prophets, it is helpful to think of this book as a prophetic comedy. It is intended to get God's reluctant witnesses then and today to laugh their way into genuine mission. Good humor is an act of worship because it is an admission of creatureliness and an implicit recognition that we creatures are not God. Humor helps us not to take ourselves too seriously. In contrast, anger is often evoked by the frustration we feel when we cannot control God or our world, which is tantamount to being frustrated that we cannot be our own gods. The main character in this Old Testament book is too angry to laugh. Faced with a nationwide revival that was the epitome of his evangelistic career, "Jonah was greatly displeased and became angry" (Jon. 4:1). God's last question in the book is intended to probe Jonah's paralyzed spirituality with words that could lead to the birth of faith, hope, and love: "Do you have a right to be angry?"

The book probes our hearts for the *real* reason why we do not share the Good News with people we do not like. It also explores the way missionaries are spiritually formed. Ironically, God's spiritual agenda is accomplished by a strategy totally foreign to today's missionary sending agencies: God calls an angry man to share a message he hardly believes with people he does not like, in order that the missionary himself might be saved. We have many missions in the world to "bad" people like the younger son in the parable of the prodigals, but this story and the New Testament counterpart (Luke 15:11-32) is a mission to good people, the people usually called to become missionaries.

Since most insiders are reluctant to relate to outsiders, the message of this book addresses the missionary vocation of the ordinary Christian. While not all Christians are gifted in evangelism, all are called to be witnesses (Acts 1:8) and to share in the every-member ministry priesthood of the people of God in declaring God's grace to the world (1 Pet. 2:9-10). Ironically, God may use the outsider to win the insider to this mission and thereby accomplish the second conversion Blumhard said we need. That appears to be God's strategy with Jonah, who is the archetypal reluctant witness. In my experience this has happened whenever I have (reluctantly, I confess) reached out to start a neighborhood Bible study or to share the message of Christ with people I meet while traveling. I start by feeling like a dispenser of God's blessings, but I almost always end up being profoundly blessed by the outsider, even if he or she never becomes a Christian.

The Archetypical Reluctant Witness

God called Jonah to evangelize the superpower threatening Israel at the time: Assyria (modern Iraq). Instead of traveling 750 miles across the desert, Jonah bought a ferry ticket and headed in the opposite direction to Tarshish (Spain) putting distance between the call of God and himself. Because God wanted this man, God ordered a big storm which provoked everyone on board to pray, everyone except Jonah, because he was asleep in the hull trying to escape from the call of God. When the sailors realized that this threatening circumstance was an exteriorization of the storm inside Jonah, they pried out the message from the reluctant messenger. They de-gospeled him. "What do you do? Where do you come from? From what people are you?"

Once I was too tired to witness, and as I slumped into the seat for a long bus ride to a distant city I said to the Lord, "No witnessing today, please!" A long-haired rock singer sat beside me to make his way to a singing engagement in the same city. He refused to be impressed with my closed eyes and my icy silence. "What do you do?" he asked.

"I teach."

"What do you teach?"

"I teach about God," I replied with as little enthusiasm as possible.

"Oh, that's interesting. Tell me more. . . . Do you know God? What is he like?"

My name is Jonah.

Jonah told them that he worshipped the God who *made* the sea, that he was running away from God, and that nothing would calm the storm but the sacrifice of the missionary. He urged them to throw him into the sea. This was his most selfless suggestion in the whole drama. But these pagan sailors risked their own lives (Jon. 1:13) to save the life of God's reluctant servant. Sometimes there is more love outside the church than inside. When all else failed they threw him overboard. Amazingly, the sea grew calm and the pagan sailors were converted to Jonah's God, even before Jonah got converted to his own God.

Converting the Missionary

Meanwhile Jonah got swallowed by a great fish and remained inside for three days and three nights, oblivious to the revival taking place on board the ship. The missionary got dumped, and the pagans got saved. If that doesn't make someone laugh, then hardly anything in heaven or on earth could.

In the great fish Jonah did not laugh, but prayed for the first time in the story. Jonah got his wish to be separated from God, but he found God in that separation, thus prefiguring the mystery of Christ's cross. Unlike one New Testament character (Luke 16:25-26), Jonah is allowed to repent *and come back*, again prefiguring the mystery that persons can be saved because Christ went through a hellish experience for us and came back. Jonah's prayer in the great fish was remarkably unselfish because Jonah found grace in God's judgment. He knew that God is *for* him. So he gave thanks and did not make a single petition (Jon. 2:1). Jonah was an almost-saved missionary.

There is more to the "sign of Jonah" (Matt. 12:38-42; Luke 11:29-32) than the mere anticipation of the historical death and resurrection of Jesus. It has to do with evangelizing missionaries, and rescuing church people from fatal narrowness. This book is placed in the Bible as a literary mission to nice people who think they already know God. No sign will convince them but this one.

Losing Control of Faith, Hope, and Love

God tried again. He regurgitated the reluctant missionary on the beach and called him a second time. Missionaries are not born, educated, or trained; they are formed in the hammer and heat of mission. The insider needs the outsider as much as the outsider needs the insider. Jonah obeyed this time because he understood that God meant business with both him and God's covenant people who had no missionary vision. But he still did not believe God meant to redeem those outside the church. Jonah preached a message of judgment as a doomsday sentence on sinners without realizing that God's judgment is always laced with hope. Albert Camus once said that he would wait resolutely for the judgment of God because he has known something far worse—the judgment of man.[2] The missionary in this case wanted outsiders to be sentenced to eternal condemnation (which they deserved), while God wanted to sentence them to eternal forgiveness (which they did not deserve). The Ninevites intuitively approached the judgment of God with more hope than Jonah did. And the king of Nineveh intuitively understood the heart of God better than the missionary did. So the king issued a prayer proclamation in the hope that "God may yet relent and with compassion turn from his fierce anger" (3:9). Ironically, it was easier for God to turn from *his* anger than the missionary to turn from his, as the next incident shows.

The pagan nation turned to Jonah's God and discovered that God meets repentance with compassion. Indeed, God's compassion inspires that repentance. Sometimes there is not only more love outside the church, but more faith and more hope. One could laugh or cry about this, or nourish a sullen submissive faith or a brooding anger like that in the heart of Jonah. "Jonah was greatly displeased and became angry" (4:1). Jonah struggled with the fact that the results of his ministry were not under his own control. He was not yet ready to laugh, or repent.

When Jonah saw that God had changed his mind about Nineveh, he changed his mind about serving God. As a last desperate attempt to defend his own theology, Jonah, like Satan, hurled revealed Scripture back at God: "I knew that you are a gracious and compassionate God" (4:2). That, he explained, is why he was so reluctant to go in the first place. He was afraid that he could not control God's response to his preaching and that God would be too soft on Israel's enemies. God's anger was not "pure" like Jonah's, or so Jonah thought. Grace bothered him. Jonah was struggling with the moral outrageousness of the Good News. And he would not make his peace with the love of God until the death and resurrection he experienced in the whale was matched by a death and resurrection in his own heart.

Jonah and the Worm

Still hoping to be vindicated before God in the end (by seeing the evil people damned) Jonah camped outside the city to see what would happen, as a geologist might camp near volcanic Mount St. Helens, hoping it would blow up while he was looking. But God is interested equally in the outsider and the insider, the pagan without the Bible and the believer with the Bible. Further, God is determined to get the outsider and the insider *together*. So God provided a vine to give shade for Jonah in the heat of the day, and then God provided a worm to attack the vine, leaving Jonah exposed to the scorching sun. God will go to almost any length to bring a person to himself. If the whale doesn't work, perhaps the worm will. Jonah's interaction with the worm was more revealing than his interaction with the whale. The worm revealed that Jonah cared for no one but himself. Jonah lived for his own righteousness, his own theology, his own ministry, and his own well-being. But he was quickly being stripped of all these possessions. Already having lost his honor as a messenger of the wrath of God, he now lost his creature comforts.

Sulking outside the city that was undergoing revival, as the older son in Jesus' parable sulked outside the kingdom party given in honor of his younger brother (Luke 15:28), Jonah wallowed in his anger, self-pity, and self-hatred. When God asked the probing question, "Do you have a right to be angry?" Jonah persisted in defending his own righteousness: "I am angry enough to die" (4:9). What, after all, is the point of living if God will not do what his messenger expects? What is the point of being a missionary if grace is unpredictable? What is the point of being in ministry if God cannot be controlled?

Losing Control of God

We are not told how the story ends. Instead we are asked a question that invites us to supply our own ending, to put ourselves into the story. "You have been concerned about this vine ... Should I not be concerned about that great city?" We, and our Old Testament counterparts, could take this story "seriously" and continue to try to keep God in our control through our own "service" and theology. Or we could laugh uproariously, positively delighting that God is still God and will not submit himself to our ministry plans or our theology.

181

No book in the Bible is more eloquent on this principle: the need is not the call. The source of mission is not the need of the world but the glory of God and God's unconditional compassion. The book of Jonah calls us to let God be God. And it powerfully suggests that if we do not let God be God, he will still be God and will continue to love the outsiders for whom we have no love.

This prophetic comedy reveals that we have a God who will convert pagans when they throw Christians overboard, a God who will vomit Christian workers out of their own private hells and send them into service a second time. In doing so God sends them to serve people who will convince the messengers of their own message. If we hear the story of Jonah and are silent, even the stones might laugh.

This book is not about a big fish, but a big God. The book invites us not to muster enough faith to believe that God could arrange to have a person swallowed and regurgitated by a big fish, but to have the greater faith that God could capture us reluctant missionaries for something larger than we dreamed: the renewal of all the world in the Messiah, Jesus.

Jonah offers a case study in missionary spirituality, not just for one reluctant prophet and his Old Testament contemporaries in 750 B.C., but for all gospel-hoarders at home or on the mission field today. If we do not recognize that our anger paralyzes authentic mission, God in his unconditional love for us may have to use pagans to break up our stony hearts. Better to double up in repentant laughter now.

PART SEVEN

A DAY OF REST

19
The Compulsive Pursuit of Leisure

"The number of places where a person can escape entertainment becomes smaller every year. . . . To restore entertainment to its proper role in society, we must restore the right to brood undisturbed."—Russell Baker

"Our present experience of eternal life should call us to question the desperate busyness which marks so many Christians. To engage in frantic activity is to become enmeshed in the time patterns of the world which will one day come to an end and is even now passing away (1 Cor. 7:29-30)."—Robert Banks

A *Time* article on "The Rat Race" suggests that "leisure could be for the '90s what money was for the '80s."[1] The article gives an accurate recital of observations about the frantic pursuit of leisure: people working harder and harder with less time to enjoy what they have earned, time-saving devices that take more of our time, the explosion of information that makes people feel like gunfighters dodging bullets, fax machines in cars, and cellular phones on vacations. We definitely have not moved into the leisure society once forecast.[2] Indeed there is good evidence to show that before the Industrial Revolution people did not work longer hours than they have since, and that modern Western people fill the time they save from work with activities that resemble work: traveling to work, maintenance of our machines and toys, shopping, gaining further education, and doing paperwork.[3] The hardest hit by the work ethic gone mad, according to this article, are the professionals. "Simply to remain competitive, professionals find that their lives are one long, continuous working day, bleeding into the wee hours and squeezing out any leisure time."[4] For many there is no day of rest.

Buying Rest

Usually, leisure is defined negatively as time free from alienating and oppressive work, and positively as time liberated for creativity, social interaction, self-realization, fantasy, and play.[5] So an exchange is made. People work for money and buy with that money the maximum experience they can for the time they have squeezed out of their hectic work week: a media experience, a gourmet meal, or an expensive vacation in an exotic get-away location. The problem, as the *Time* article revealed, is that when we get there we have brought our work with us.

"My wife and I were sitting on the beach in Anguilla on one of our rare vacations," recalls architect Trunzo, "and even there my staff was able to reach me. There are times," he reflects, "when our lives are clearly leading us."[6]

Many people say they have to get back to work to feel "rested" again! "Leisure," Gordon Dahl says, "has come to mean little more than an ever more furious orgy of consumption. . . . This 'virtuous materialism' . . . offers men the choice of either working themselves to death or consuming themselves to death—or both."[7] The day of rest has become another day of work.

The Toxic Mix

What makes the frantic pursuit of leisure so pointless is that we bring into it the same drivenness that infects our work. People who push figures all day compulsively jog, watch television, or ski when they are not working. The problem goes deep into our souls. We are restless whenever we function in response to neurotic needs from inside rather than the call of God from outside. Typically the driven person was raised in a nonaffirming environment in which love was conditional on performance. He or she usually experienced deprivation or shame early in life, and was raised in an environment where drivenness was a way of life.[8] Gordon Macdonald offers the intriguing, though misleading, suggestion that "Paul the apostle in his pre-Christian days was driven . . . until Christ called him."[9] But Paul's holy zeal and sanctified ambition was not the mere conversion of his "type A" personality or the sanctification of his neuroses. It was the response of his whole person to live for the praise of God's glory (Eph. 1:12) with all the energy God so mightily inspired in him (Col. 1:29). There is no day of rest for a driven person. Every day can be a day of rest for the called person.

Christian Pseudo-Sabbath

But even the attempt to experience Sabbath can become work. The Church unwittingly encourages the toxic mix of compulsive ministry and utilitarian spirituality. Good Christians are active in the Church and are known for their sacrificial activity rather than their experience of rest. The "best" ministers are usually workaholics. Even nonprofessional church and parachurch workers can be so addicted to ministry that they can never retire from it or make place for another. Hardly ever is a person commended for refusing an office. *Doing* is considered more important than *being*. Sunday is often the most hectic and stressful day of the week, the least restful.

Our personal devotional life, too, has been inflicted with our passion for productivity. As Kenneth Leech so wisely observed, what spoils so much of our spiritual life is that we insist it be useful and productive. We bring utilitarianism into it. Whereas the work of Sabbath rest is precisely the opposite. It is *otium*—(true) leisure or rest, peace—the blessing of Sabbath.[10]

Leisure and Sabbath

Instead of offering a spirituality of leisure as opposed to work, the Bible offers Sabbath, which includes much more than leisure and does not exclude work. Leisure is usually defined *over and against work*. So defined it is implicitly bound to its opposite—work. It is what one does when one is free from work to recuperate from work and therefore can offer only a limited rest *from* work. Leisure offers no rest *in* work. Sabbath, in contrast, is not merely an alternative to work. It is not restricted to free time but is extended to cover the whole of time.

Sabbath and leisure have much in common: they are both personally restorative, enjoyable, nonutilitarian, and playful. But there are significant differences. Leisure is a matter of personal choice; Sabbath is a divine law (Exod. 20:8). Leisure is perceived as avocational; Sabbath is vocational—part of the response of our entire persons to the call of God. Leisure is directed mainly to self, while Sabbath is directed more to God. Therefore leisure is more concerned with pleasure than meaning, while Sabbath is more concerned with meaning than pleasure. Both are aesthetic, but leisure tends toward hedonism, while Sabbath invites contemplation. In sum, leisure is more often a diversion from Sabbath than a means of experiencing Sabbath, and thus I think it reasonable to call it pseudo-Sabbath. It cannot give us a day of rest. But this idea is so unpopular that we must explore it more deeply.

20
Playing Heaven

"Of all ridiculous things, it seems to me the most ridiculous is to be a busy man of affairs, prompt to meals, and prompt to work. Hence when I see a fly settled down in a crucial moment on the nose of a businessman, or see him bespattered by a carriage which passes by him in even greater haste, or a draw-bridge opens before him or a tile from the roof falls down and strikes him dead, then I laugh heartily. And who could help laughing? What do they accomplish, these hustlers? Are they not like the housewife, when her house was on fire, who in her excitement saved the fire-tongs? What more do they save from the great fire of life?"
—*Søren Kierkegaard*

"Prayer is an experience of gratuity. This 'pointless' act, this 'squandered' time, reminds us that the Lord is beyond being categorized as useful or useless."—*Gustavo Gutierrez*

The huge leisure industry offers us pseudo-Sabbath. It reduces leisure to a commodity that insists we focus on ourselves and keeps us earth-bound. It seduces us into believing that our avocations are more attractive and meaningful than our vocations.[1] But if we believe this, we find ourselves internally divided, stressed, and restless. So we work at play and do not even play playfully.

Sabbath Leisure

Earlier I suggested that there is not what may properly be called a doctrine of leisure in the Bible.[2] But there is a theology of Sabbath leisure. It has at least four dimensions. First, there is the creational ordinance of *rest*—weekly (Exod. 20:8-11; Exod. 31:13-17; Deut. 5:12-15; Isa. 58:13-14), yearly, every seventh year, and even a jubilee rest for the land and the people (Lev. 25:8-55). This creational ordinance takes us beyond the mere observance of a day to envision the three-fold harmony of God, humankind, and creation. Second, there is a *playfulness and wastefulness* built into God's creation: millions of seeds that never germinate; leaves that turn into brilliant colors and die; and flowers that display their beauty even when no one is looking. Some of God's creation is non-utilitarian, useless. Nevertheless it is there to be enjoyed—by God, if no one else is looking! Surprisingly, when God speaks to Job out of the whirlwind, he does not give a theological answer to Job's searching questions. Rather, in Job 38–39 he reflects on how much he enjoys his own creation even though much of it goes unobserved or unused by humankind. This contemplative passage contains the deep truth that God enjoys being God![3] God describes entering his own rest (Gen. 2:2) and enjoying his own creation once again as he reflects in the hearing of the astonished Job, "Who cuts a channel for the torrents of rain, and a path for the thunderstorm, to water a land *where no man lives,* a desert with no one in it, to satisfy a desolate wasteland and make it sprout with grass?" (Job 38:25-27, emphasis mine).

Third, there is *a tradition of festivity* in the whole Bible, especially in the Old Testament. Pilgrimages were like camping trips, and pilgrims to Jerusalem were encouraged to exchange their tithes, composed of fruit and animals, for money that could be taken to Jerusalem (Deut. 14:24-26). Once at the Holy City they could use their tithes to buy "cattle, sheep, wine or other fermented drink, *or anything you wish. Then you and your household shall eat there in the presence of the Lord your God and rejoice"* (14:26, emphasis mine). Finally, there is the *affirmation of godly pleasure* not only in the enigmatic confessions of the Preacher/Professor (Ecclesiastes) but also in the *Song of Songs,* which is a meditation on the joy of sex-play between marriage partners and an exposition of Adam's expectant joy when first he met Eve as expressed himself in a praise-poem: "Here, at last!" (See Gen. 2:23). Sexual intercourse is a form of marital Sabbath.[4] And it is precisely the demand to perform or the fear of performing inadequately that reduces sexual intercourse in many marriages to a boring ritual or an area of conflict.[5]

Holy Play

Play is not merely "the pause that refreshes"—Johnston calls this the "Protestant viewpoint"[6]—but it is good for its own sake. God himself "played" when he made the world. Wisdom that was from eternity before the world began (Prov. 8:23) played in the Father's presence when the world was created: "Then I was the craftsman at his side. I was filled with delight day after day, rejoicing always in his presence, rejoicing in his whole world and delighting in mankind" (8:30-31). Similarly God tells Job that the world and humankind are the fruit of heavenly, playful love "while the morning stars sang together and all the angels shouted for joy" (Job 38:7). All human beings are love babies. We were not created for the utilitarian purpose of getting work done on earth from God's perspective. Rather, we were created as the fruit of God's own love. In the same way, the universe is the result of continuous covenant love between the Father, Son, and Holy Spirit (John 17:5, 23). The playfulness of this is hard for us to grasp because for adults play and work have been tragically separated, whereas for children they are one experience.

Children, according to Robert Johnston, have "un-adulterated" play![7] For children, work and play are a single experience. Children at play are free from instrumentality, from gauging their results. The inner world of children at play is unhampered by any need to feel productive. Through the dreadful process of growing up children learn that persons should be defined by what they do, that work is more important than play, that relationships must "work," that even prayer must produce results. Children ask their parents, "Will you play with me?" In one sense nothing is accomplished by such play, but in reality something crucial *is* achieved: parent and child mutually affirm that they enjoy and prize each other.[8] As we grow up we make this terrible separation between work and play. With God, Walter Ong says in the forward of *Man At Play*, "such separation never comes. God's work is always play in the sense that it is always joyous, spontaneous and completely free."[9] Playfulness and holiness should be inseparable.

In his book *Man At Play* Hugh Rahner recovers an old allegory that was used by Philo of Alexandria to convey his thoughts about the playfulness of the holy life.[10] The allegory is based on Genesis 26:8, where Abimilech, who had been told that Rebekah was Isaac's sister rather than his wife, observes Isaac "playing" with his wife. The Hebrew word clearly suggests sex-play, as represented in the older translations by the words "sporting with." But the Alexandrian commentators saw more than "foreplay" in the text; they remembered that Isaac's name meant "laughter" (Gen. 21:6), while Rebekah's name means "perseverance." King Abimelech, they said, knew Isaac and Rebekah were husband and wife, and not merely brother and sister, because laughter and perseverance are a wedded pair. So, say the commentators, *homo ludens* must unite gaiety and patience, and the child's play of man is heavenly. The godly person is, according to Philo, "full of heartsease and joy."[11]

Whether it is verbal play, aesthetic play, or athletic play, there is a deep truth hidden in our use of language. Athletes "play" the game, and musicians "play" their instruments. The best workers know how to play at it. Even more important is to know why.

Justified Play

In *Thank God It's Monday* William Diehl remarks that the biggest gap between our confessed theology of Sunday (that we are saved by grace through faith, and not by our works) and our experience of Monday, is works righteousness. On Sunday we discover we are justified by grace through faith in Jesus (Gal. 1:16). On Monday, he argues, "our actions betray a belief that our identity and worth are based entirely on what we do and how well we do it."[12] Perhaps our inability to play and our struggle to experience the holy leisure of Sabbath is related to lack of working "in" the salvation God has worked "out" in history. We have not yet been liberated from having to accomplish, having to work, having to perform for God. And so we work at play. We even work at keeping Sabbath, rather than letting the Sabbath keep us.

On this point the penetrating work by Jurgen Moltmann is very helpful. He argues that Israel was given two archetypal images of liberation: the Exodus and the Sabbath, one being the symbol of external freedom and the other being the symbol of internal freedom. Exodus and Sabbath, Moltmann maintains, belong together. The playfulness and "uselessness" of the Sabbath is related to the objective accomplishment of God's saving work in history as witnessed in the Exodus.[13] So, argues Moltmann, keeping the Sabbath is the freedom from striving to "prove" that one is saved or that one has to accomplish something in this world to be accepted by God. He continues:

Sanctifying the sabbath means being entirely free from striving for happiness and from the will for performance and achievement. It means being wholly present in the presence of God. The sabbath is sanctified through God alone. *The peace of the sabbath can be viewed as the Jewish "doctrine of justification."* Anyone who looks at Israel on the sabbath cannot reproach her with a "righteousness of works." And on the other hand, Christian faith in justification must be understood analogously as "the sabbath rest" of Christians.[14]

So from the very beginning God had in mind that people would enjoy him, enjoy his creation, and even enjoy themselves! Sabbath was designed as a playful day that would call forth faith. It is an opportunity to reflect leisurely on Creation (Exod. 20:11) and salvation (Deut. 5:15). Sabbath is sheer unadulterated grace—child's play.

Eden Play

Sabbath is the climax of the week. Significantly, in the creation story Adam and Eve were created on the sixth day, ready for rest on the seventh (Gen. 2:2-3). Adam and Eve woke up to experience Sabbath, not to get on with their work. Sabbath was their first experience in the world. A week later, in resting from gardening and community-building in paradise, Adam and Eve were "playing" God; they were imagining God in their creaturely selves as they brooded on the week's work and play. God also works and rests (Gen. 2:2), and as regents, kingly representatives, we imitate God in both. So we honor God with our work *and* our play.

Creation is *for* the covenant. And the covenant is *for* creativity. Joy is the goal of Creation, and unmitigated joy is the unmistakable mark of the presence of God. Sabbath should be marked by that joy.

Heavenly Play

One of the greatest and most revolutionary claims of Jesus is to be Lord even of the Sabbath (Mark 2:28). To demonstrate this claim Jesus worked and played on Saturday while he pointed to the full and final presence of his kingdom. He dared to offer Sabbath rest in his own person (Matt. 11:28), inaugurating a threefold harmony of God, humankind, and Creation through his own person and work. He offers not merely personal salvation but Sabbath. Rather than transgressing Sabbath, as was charged against him, or abolishing Sabbath, as is sometimes thought by Christians, Jesus fulfilled Sabbath. He could not be the kingdom of God in his own person without fulfilling Sabbath by bringing peace, forgiveness, healing, liberation, and hope as prophesied before (Isa. 61).[15]

In the New Testament, the Sabbath experienced in Jesus foreshadows the heavenly paradise, where work and rest will be one glorious experience in the ultimate garden city, the New Jerusalem (Heb. 4:1-11). Our experience of Sabbath now, as followers of Jesus, is "playing heaven." Just as children imitate their parents and "play house," believers imitate their heavenly Father by anticipating and preparing for the ultimate environment that God has prepared for us. May we not also view Sabbath as a way of "playing" with God, celebrating the mutual delight God and we, his covenant partners, have in each other and the work we do together?

This seems implied in crucial Sabbath passages in Genesis 1–2. They show us that *being* is more important than *doing*. As Moltmann says,

> Existence precedes activity. So activity ends in simply being present. . . . The celebration of the sabbath leads to an intensified capacity for perceiving the loveliness of everything—food, clothing, the body, the soul—because existence itself is glorious. Questions about the possibility

of "producing" something, or about utility, are forgotten in the face of the beauty of all created things, which have their meaning simply in their very selves.[16]

My colleague Loren Wilkinson put it this way: "Making is important, for both God and man. But even more important is to rest in what is made—to delight in it."[17] Perhaps we would do a better job of looking after the earth if we spent the time of our lives playing heaven, at least one day a week, and possibly every day.

21

Reinventing Sabbath

"There is a realm of time where the goal is not to have but to be, not to own but to give, not to control but to share, not to subdue but to be in accord."—Abraham Heschel

"Six days a week we live under the tyranny of things in space; on the Sabbath we try to become attuned to holiness in time. It is a day on which we are called upon to share what is eternal in time, to turn from the results of creation to the mystery of creation; from the world of creation to the creation of the world."—Abraham Heschel

In the deepest sense, we do not keep Sabbath; the Sabbath keeps us. Sabbath was intended to be the leisured but intentional experience of reflection on the source and goals of our life on earth. Therefore, it keeps us turned toward God and heaven-bound. So we make ourselves available to the gift of Sabbath precisely because we are not capable on our own of sustaining our orientation toward God and our heavenly direction. So we are left with a biblical irony: we must labor to enter that rest (Heb. 4:11). In this final chapter we must explore how to enter that rest. Some form of Sabbath is not an optional extra for the New Testament Christian. It is fundamental to spiritual health, and even to emotional health.[1]

Experiencing Special-Day Sabbath

Keeping one day as a special day of reflection on the meaning of the other six is increasingly more difficult in a secularized society that now exploits Sunday as the ultimate day for shopping and leisure activities. For pastors Sunday is a work day, and I recommend for them keeping a Jewish Sabbath: Friday sundown to Saturday sundown. When I was a pastor I found that the Lord always honored my prayer that my Sunday sermon would be ready by Friday supper. That way I could rest when my family was resting. Very involved laypersons with heavy responsibilities on Sunday must either reduce their stressful activities to one portion of Sunday or choose another day for Sabbath.

Each person will find a pattern that fits, at least for a while. Different occupational experiences and changes in family responsibilities will cause us to adjust our pattern from time to time. A friend of mine spends every Thursday in the lounge of a first-class hotel nearby reading his Bible and Christian classics. Personally, I find two complete days every two or three weeks are most suitable for me. I take these days away from the telephone and the workplace and spend them any way I wish. Sometimes I spend time walking or watching a sunset. Sometimes I like to build something.

Often these special-day Sabbaths are splendid opportunities to follow one of the many spiritual disciplines we have explored in "A Day Alone," disciplines that have enriched the spirituality of the church over the centuries: Bible meditation, confession, waiting prayer, intercession for others. An excellent guide for this is *The Celebration of Discipline* by Richard Foster. A whole book of the Bible can be read at one sitting, or a single verse can become the subject of meditation for several hours.

Sabbath is also an ideal time for the journey inward, exploring what Thoreau called "the Atlantic and Pacific of one's own being alone." Very active people need to stop long enough to let their soul catch up to their bodies. An old Arab saying is that a person's soul can travel as fast as a camel. If that is true, then some of us need to stop still for a long time to get connected. Religion, in the true meaning of the word, is that which binds together, so making us whole. When we create space and time to be real with God important questions often surface, questions that could lead to more connectedness.

Every two or three years on one of these retreats, I intentionally "walk through my life with Jesus," praying that he will show me how *he* sees the experiences of my childhood, youth, and adulthood. This usually takes several hours but is an important experience in my viewing my life experiences from his point of view (2 Cor. 5:16). Far from being simple introspection—itself a fruitless if not depressing activity—talking to God about ourselves is healing. All the journeys—upward, outward, and inward—are interrelated. In exploring spiritual disciplines we do so not as a religious activity, something *done* for God to seek his acceptance. Amateurs do it for love. They know themselves as sought and found by the seeking Father (John 4:23). For true lovers it does not matter very much what they do when they are together, just as long as they are together. The disciplines are not important. They are simply paths of removing obstacles to make ourselves more freely available to the seeking Father.

I have, until now, been exploring an individual use of Sabbath as a special day. I have done so deliberately because I am convinced that one can only afford to be in Christian community if one has learned how to be alone with God. Otherwise we tend to feed parasitically on the corporate life of the church. But now I must offer a word about Sabbath as a church. I have come to believe that worship together is the most important thing we do in the gathered life of the church. If Sabbath is being liberated from the tyranny of productivity and performance to rediscover our identities through love, then worship is an obvious way to keep the Sabbath. We do not worship for what *we* get out of it. That would bring our utilitarian work ethic into worship. Ironically, praise "works" precisely because it lifts us above our compulsion to make everything useful. It is mere enjoyment of God, nothing more, nothing less. C. S. Lewis once said that in *commanding* us to worship him, God is *inviting* us to worship him.

Significantly when Vladimir, Prince of Kiev, while still a pagan, desired to know which was the true religion, and sent his followers to various countries of the world, they found no joy. But when they journeyed to Constantinople and attended the divine liturgy in St. Sophia they exclaimed, "We knew not whether we were in heaven or on earth."[2]

I think of worship as "playing heaven." In heaven, space and time are both gloriously redeemed. Therefore we will be occupied primarily with worship. Far from being dull or stereotyped, the worship pictured in Revelation 21–22 is space and time spent in exquisite beauty and filled with creative experiences. Sight, sound, and movement are all centered on Christ, the Lamb. All our worship on earth is like a grand rehearsal, worth doing for its own sake, but intended to prepare for a grander occasion. Sabbath-days help us to "play heaven." But what about making every day Sabbath, the second Pauline model?

Every Day a Holy Day

Perhaps the apostle Paul had the *kairos-chronos* distinction in mind when he reinterpreted the Old Testament Sabbath law. He said, "One man considers one day more sacred than another; another man considers every day alike. Each one should be fully convinced in his own mind" (Rom. 14:5). To make absolutely clear that he was not saying that Sabbath is now *optional* he continues: "He who regards one day as special, does so *to the Lord . . . for none of us lives to himself alone . . ."* (14:6-7). Sabbath can now be one day or *every* day, *or both.*

Paul was not original in this idea but was merely expounding the words and deeds of Jesus. In Jesus' day, Sabbath-observance had been reduced to a task, a work to be performed. The religious people of his day were trying to squeeze *kairos* out of *chronos* by hedging the day with a myriad of prohibitions to make it happen or to protect it from becoming secular. So the day came to be served both for its own sake and for the merit people obtained in "doing it just right." In contrast, Jesus viewed Sabbath as something given by God for man's benefit, not something man served: "The Sabbath was made for man, not man for the Sabbath" (Mark 2:27).[3] Jesus regarded himself Lord even of the Sabbath. He demonstrated his lordship over time by delighting his Father in how he spent the day. He *enjoyed* the day by doing what his Father loves to do on the Sabbath: creating and recreating, resting and bringing rest to others. He healed the sick, an unheard-of activity that the Pharisees considered to be prohibited work. But for Jesus it was a form of rest in the Father's presence and power. Mark shrewdly observes that the plot to assassinate Jesus was hatched after one such healing, the leaders were so offended (Mark 3:6)—an observation amplified by John (John 5:18). It is hard to resist the conclusion, given the number of miracles Jesus worked on the Sabbath, that Jesus deliberately chose to do most of his healings on Saturday! He had a point to make: Sabbath is not the absence of work but experiencing the joy of God, ceasing to do one's own work, entering into God's work. The author of the Letter to the Hebrews had this same thought: "for any one who enters God's rest also rests from his own work, just as God did from his . . . make every effort to enter that rest" (Heb. 4:10-11). This author hints that entering Sabbath is, ironically, hard work for us because we are so driven to make Sabbath a personal performance, a thing we make happen, rather than a delicious relaxation in God. Sabbath becomes the model of salvation.

Most Christians find that whether or not they have kept a special day, they need a time especially dedicated to God every day, generally in the morning. Women with small children may find another time of day more profitable, and husbands can care for children during this time to give a "Sabbath gift" to their spouse. Personally, I have not found a better resource for this than McCheyne's lectionary with its schedule for reading through the Old Testament once each year and the New Testament and Psalms twice.[4] The advantage of this plan is that one reads consecutively in four parts of the Bible at the same time. Usually people get stuck in Leviticus when they try to read from Genesis to Revelation.

But it is important to explore the reason for a daily quiet time. I have already mentioned the most important, namely, that the Father is seeking us. Spiritual disciplines are not ways of finding God or attaining sanctification, but chasing away obstacles that keep us from being continuously found by God. It is a mighty work on our part to make ourselves truly available to God. The farmer cannot make the seeds grow, but he must work hard in cultivating the soil. That is what daily Sabbath involves. There is a further reason.

Our society continuously inundates us with messages to buy, to consume, and to experience. It is impossible to be unaffected by the ubiquitous appeal of the advertising world to the flesh. That is reason enough to spend time each day in a mini-Sabbath. But the purpose is not merely to "bank" good thoughts before we are besieged by greed, pride, sex, and violence in the world out there. The purpose is to shape just how we are to live. It seems imperative to me that persons committed to making every day Sabbath must learn how to *reduce* the stimulation they receive from society. They will see fewer movies, watch less television, and monitor more carefully what they read. "We are what we eat" is the one-liner in the gastronomic world, and "We are what we see and hear" is a partial truth in the realm of the soul. We want to live each hour for God, in his presence seeking his pleasure.

I am actually making an unpopular proposal. I am suggesting that if we adopt a Sabbath lifestyle we will have less need for leisure activities and "diversions." The world offers work and leisure. The Bible offers work and Sabbath. Leisure and Sabbath are not necessarily the same thing. Sabbath involves the threefold harmony of God, humankind, and Creation. Prayer and Bible reading are part of this. But so may be digging a garden or making a model boat or trying a new recipe. For a full experience of Sabbath we will contemplate Creation, redemption, and our complete consummation in heaven. If we truly experience Sabbath we will have fun, be playful, and be deeply joyful, whether or not we do all the fun things offered by society. Indeed leisure can become a diversion *from* Sabbath, and an unsatisfying one at that.

Sometimes what people need most to make every day Sabbath is to see that they get a good night's sleep *every* night, so far as it is possible. As the *Time* article suggested, most people in North America are constantly tired—and no wonder, given the frantic work and leisure schedule. God literally refreshes his beloved daily in sleep (Ps. 4:8; 127:1-2).[5] Refreshed in sleep and renewed by our exposure to the life-giving power of Scripture and prayer, we can face the demands of work.

Once again, a Sabbath lifestyle makes work an opportunity to experience the presence of God as rest. In *The Practice of the Presence of God* we discover how Brother Lawrence made it his practice to do everything he did for the love of God, seeking only God's pleasure and approval. Thus he found that the least or greatest task did not divert him from God. "With him the set times of prayer were not different from other times . . . because his greatest business did not divert him from God."[6] He went to God *through* all the dimensions of his day. This was all the more extraordinary in that he had a natural aversion to the job he had—working in a monastery kitchen. In so doing the earthly realities of our everyday life become *transparent*.

We have explored an almost-forgotten perspective crucial to the Christian lifestyle. Rediscovering Sabbath is one way of learning to put *being* before *doing* and to recover an authentic spirituality. It delivers our spiritual life from the pollutant of utilitarianism, the passion to be useful. Sabbath is wasted time, but holy waste to be redeemed in God's own way in God's own time. Vincent van Gogh, a true amateur, wrote to his brother Theo these words about a day of rest:

There may be a great fire in our soul, yet no one ever comes to warm himself at it, and the passers-by only see a wisp of smoke coming through the chimney, and go along their way. Look here, now, what must be done? Must one tend the inner fire, have salt in oneself, wait patiently yet with how much impatience for the hour when somebody will come and sit down near it—maybe to stay? Let him who believes in God wait for the hour that will come sooner or later.[7]

Epilogue: The Eighth Day of Creation

"Jesus' proclamation of the imminent kingdom makes the whole of life a sabbath feast."—Jurgen Moltmann

"What he ordains for us each moment is what is most holy, best and most divine for us."—Jean-Pierre Caussade

Our meditation on the spirituality of the ordinary Christian has been structured around seven days. But a curious phrase was used in the second century in the Epistle of Barnabas: "the eighth day."

In this primitive Christian document, Barnabas looks forward to an ultimate fulfillment of Sabbath when the Son of Man comes. Speaking for God, Barnabas says, "The present sabbaths are not acceptable to me, but that which I have made, in which I will give rest to all things and make *the beginning of an eighth day, that is the beginning of another world.* Wherefore we also celebrate with gladness the eighth day in which Jesus also rose from the dead, and was made manifest, and ascended into Heaven."[1] So it is with good reason that the Russian theologian Berdyaev spoke of the event of Easter as the eighth day of creation.[2] What was created at the beginning, all that we are and have, and all the days of the week, enter at Easter into the beginning of the glorification of everything. Robert Markus draws upon an Augustinian thought to reflect on baptism as the rite that "introduces the Christian into the new life of the age to come, and hence also into the new order of work where the gulf between toil and rest is closed."[3]

The Christian vocation is to conquer space and sanctify time, and we do this by living completely in this world for Jesus, who is the firstborn of Creation and the firstborn from the dead. But because the eighth day has begun we live simultaneously both *in* this world and *for* the coming world. The transfiguration of everything has begun.

The purpose of keeping one day a week or one hour a day especially for God is to set us up for redeeming all the time of our lives: all seven days. Heschel speaks very eloquently and evocatively about this: "The Sabbath is an example of the world to come. . . ."[4] "The essence of the world to come is Sabbath eternal, and the seventh day in time is an example of eternity."[5]

"We usually think," Heschel suggests, "that the earth is our mother, that time is money and profit our mate. The seventh day is a reminder that God is our father, that time is life and the spirit is our mate."[6] Heschel recites the story of a rabbi who once entered heaven in his dream. He was permitted to approach the temple in Paradise where the great sages of the Talmud, the Tannaim, were spending their eternal lives. He saw that they were just sitting around tables studying the Talmud. The disappointed rabbi wondered, "Is this all there is to Paradise?" But suddenly he heard a voice: "You are mistaken. The Tannaim are not in Paradise. Paradise is in the Tannaim."[7]

In the Jewish context Heschel says, "Judaism tries to foster the vision of life as a pilgrimage to the seventh day; the longing for the Sabbath all the days of the week which is a form of longing for the eternal sabbath all the days of our lives."[8] As we have seen, for the Christian this requires both of the Pauline models of Sabbath: one special day and an every-day Sabbath. All seven days are a pilgrimage toward the eighth day of creation—the full experience of the transfiguration of everything in Jesus Christ. This life in all of its earthy, sweaty, joyful, and ecstatic reality—work, family, sexuality, brothers and sisters, aloneness, neighbors, and rest—can be seen transparently in the light of the resurrection life of Jesus. All seven days are holy because the eighth day is dawning.

Notes

Introduction

1. Dietrich Bonhoeffer's idea of "religionless Christianity" has sparked extensive debate since it was expounded (perhaps incorrectly) in Bishop Robinson's controversial *Honest to God*. But as Claude J. Geffre says, "Even if we must criticize all the ambiguities of a systematic opposition between faith and religion, the fact remains that the question put by Bonhoeffer is a real one when he asks how we should proclaim the God of Jesus Christ to a man who has not been preconditioned by religion" ("Desacralization and the Spiritual Life," *Concilium* 19 [1966], 125).

2. Leonard Doohan, *The Lay-Centered Church: Theology and Spirituality* (Minneapolis, Minn.: Winston Press, 1984), 43.

3. John Redekop, "Christian Labour—A Place for Christians?" *Faith Today* (September/October 1989), 18-23.

4. Quoted in Donald Bloesch, *Crisis in Piety* (Grand Rapids, Mich.: Eerdmans, 1968), 102.

5. *Lumen Gentium*, 24 and 32. This very ancient idea appears in some of John Chrysostom's sermons *In Genesim Sermones*, 6, 2, P.G., 54, 607-608, and *Epist, ad Ephes.* V, 20, P.G., 62, 143-144.

6. Karl Rahner, "Marriage as a Sacrament," *Theological Investigations* (New York: Seabury, 1973), p. 221, quoted in Eugene J. Fisher, "Perspectives on the Family in Christian and Jewish Traditions," *Service International de Documentation Judeo-Chretienne—SIDIC* (1981), 14:4-15.

7. See Dolores Leckey, *The Ordinary Way: A Family Spirituality* (New York: Crossroad Books, 1982).

8. Richard Rohr, "An Appetite for Wholeness: Living with Our Sexuality," *Sojourners* (November 1982), 30.

9. Dietrich Bonhoeffer, *Life Together*, John W. Doberstein, trans. (New York: Harper and Row, 1954), 26-30.

10. Walter Hilton, *Toward a Perfect Love: The Spiritual Counsel of Walter Hilton*, David L. Jeffrey, trans. (Portland, Oreg.: Multnomah Press, 1985), 86.

11. David L. Jeffrey, trans., in Walter Hilton, *Letters to a Layman*, in *Toward a Perfect Love*, op. cit., xxi.

12. Jose-Maria Gonzalez-Ruiz, "Spirituality for a Time of Uncertainty," *Concilium* 19 (1966), 69.

13. Gustavo Gutiérrez, *A Theology of Liberation* (Maryknoll: Orbis Books, 1973), 206, quoted in Jon Sobrino, "Christian Prayer and New Testament Theology: A Basis for Social Justice and Spirituality" in Matthew Fox, ed., *Western Spirituality* (Sante Fe: Bear and Co., 1981), 79.

14. Abraham Joshua Heschel, *The Earth Is the Lord's and The Sabbath* (New York: Harper and Row, 1951), 4-6.

15. Ibid., 3.

16. Ibid., 10.

17. Robert Bultot, "The Theology of Earthly Realities and Lay Spirituality," *Concilium* 19 (1966), 44.

18. Kenneth Leech, *True Prayer: An Invitation to Christian Spirituality* (San Francisco: Harper and Row, 1980), 79.

19. Clement of Alexandria, *Strom*, VII, 3, 18, 2, GCS 17, 13, quoted in Alfons Auer, *Open to the World: An Analysis of Lay Spirituality*, Dennis Doherty, trans. (Baltimore, M.D.: Helican Press, 1966), 20.

20. Dietrich Bonhoeffer in a letter from Tegel prison, 1944, quoted in Melanie Morrison, "As One Who Stands Convicted," *Sojourners* (May 1979), 15.

21. Catherine De Hueck Doherty, *The People of the Towel and the Water* (Denville, N.J.: Dimension Books, 1978), 8.

22. James Houston, "Do the Works of Men Secularize the Service of Christ," *Interchange*, 62.

23. Alexander M. Witherspoon, ed., *The College Survey of English Literature* (New York: Harcourt, Brace and Co., 1951), 661.

24. William Blake, *A Vision of the Last Judgement*, 92-95, emphasis mine.

25. Auer, op. cit., 230, italics mine.

Chapter One/Faith: Discovering the Soul of Work

1. Bonhoeffer, op. cit., 70.

2. Most of the foregoing appeared first as an article in *The Regent World* (May 1990), and was later published in *Marketplace* (January 1992).

3. Gustaf Wingren, *Luther on Vocation*, Carl C. Rasmussen, trans. (St. Louis, Mo.: Concordia, 1957), 143.

4. Calvin Seerveld, *Christian Workers, Unite!* (Toronto, Ont.: Christian Labour Association of Canada [90 Hadrian Drive, Rexdale, Ontario], 1964), 7-8.

Chapter Two/Love: Recovering the Amateur Status of the Christian

1. George MacDonald, *The Genius of Willie MacMichael* (Wheaton, Ill.: Victor Books, 1987), 18-20.

2. David L. Jeffrey, trans. Walter Hilton, *Toward a Perfect Love*, op. cit., xxv.

3. William J. Dumbrell, *Creation and Covenant* (Nashville, Tenn.: Thomas Nelson, 1984), 38.

4. Though the idea of co-creativity has been co-opted by such authors as Teilhard de Chardin, Gibson Winter, Matthew Fox, and Thomas Berry, and fits the postmodern cultural framework of the day with its ecological-mystical reformulation of religious traditions, it would be tragic to label all thoughts of co-creativity as "New Age" or "post-modernism." There are, however, some dangers. One Christian author, Joe Holland, seems to lose sight of the biblical perspectives of the transcendence and immanence of God and comes dangerously close to deifying human creativity and diminishing God's. But he makes the important point that "Jesus's gospel speaks to the work process not because he grew up in a carpenter's family but because he proclaims a new creation" (Joe Holland, *Creative Communion: Toward a Spirituality of Work* [New York: Paulist Press, 1989], 58).

5. Lee Hardy, *The Fabric of This World* (Grand Rapids, Mich.: Eerdmans, 1990), 48.

6. The medieval definition of *sloth* as one of the seven deadly sins was "too much" as well as "too little" work!

7. Martin Luther, "Treatise on Good Works," W.A. Lambert, trans., James Atkinson, ed., *Luther's Works*, vol. 44 (Philadelphia: Fortress Press, 1966), 26-27.

Chapter Three/Hope: Making Our Mark on Heaven

1. Lesslie Newbigin, *Honest Religion for Secular Man* (Philadelphia: Westminster Press, 1966), 146.

2. Aristotle, *Politics*, I.viii.9; *Nichomachean Ethics*, X.7.

3. Edward Vanderkloet, "Why Work Anyway? The Work Ethic in History," *The Guide* (January/February 1978), 6.

4. The curse on work in Genesis 3:17-19 should be distinguished from the Greek view. In Genesis, work—which was intrinsically good—has been spoiled by sin. This led to frustration and resultlessness. The Greek view, however, suggested that work was innately shameful and dishonorable. It was something done by slaves and had no implicit dignity.

5. Gordon D. Fee, *The First Epistle to the Corinthians*, The New International Commentary on the New Testament, F.F. Bruce, ed. (Grand Rapids, Mich.: Eerdmans, 1987), 321-322.

6. This dictum has been ascribed to Luther, but it is an apocryphon. It may stem from a grenadier of Frederick II of Prussia. Quoted by Markus Barth, *Ephesians, Translation and Commentary on Chapters 4-6*, vol. 34A, The Anchor Bible (Garden City, N.Y.: Doubleday, 1981), 517.

7. John Haughey, *Converting Nine to Five: A Spirituality of Daily Work* (New York: Crossroads, 1989), 106.

8. Lynn White, *Science* 155, March 10, 1967, no. 3767, 1203-1207.

9. J. B. Lightfoot, *Saint Paul's Epistles to the Colossians and to Philemon*, rev. ed. (Grand Rapids, Mich.: Eerdmans, 1879), 156.

10. Haughey, op. cit., 104.

11. It is possible that the meaning of "The heavens will disappear with a roar; the elements will be destroyed by fire, and the earth and everything in it will be laid bare (or burned up)" (2 Pet. 3:10) is not the total annihilation of the cosmos but the purifying of the created order as ore in a smelter.

Chapter Four/Domestic Spirituality

1. Robert Frost, "Death of a Hired Hand," *The Poems of Robert Frost* (New York: Random House, 1946), 41-42.

2. Ernest Boyer, Jr., *Finding God at Home: Family Life as Spiritual Discipline* (San Francisco: Harper and Row, 1984), xiii.

3. This anonymous article was printed in the University Chapel newsletter (Sunday, May 10, 1992), Vancouver, B.C.

4. Stan Skarsten, "The Family: Unchanged and Changing," *Crux*, vol. 6, no. 4 (August 1969), 22.

5. Lesley Francis, "Crisis in the Family," *Vancouver Sun* (Saturday, January 5, 1991), section C, p. 1. See also "What Happened to the Traditional Family?" in *Context: Research to Make Religion Relevant* (Spring 1991) (Mississauga, Ont.: MARC Canada, a division of World Vision Canada).

6. R.D. Laing, *The Politics of Experience and the Bird of Paradise* (Harmondsworth, England: Penguin Books, 1970), 55.

7. Michael Novak, "Family Out of Favour," *Harpers* (April 1976), 44.

8. Ibid., 39.

9. Peter and Brigitte Berger, *The War Over the Family: Capturing the Middle Ground* (Garden City, NY: Anchor Press, 1984), 109-110.

10. When my wife and I travel in Africa I am always called by my family name, and Gail is sometimes known as "the wife of the Bald One." Most people in rural

areas are reticent to acknowledge their given or "Christian" name, since one makes oneself vulnerable to being known, controlled, and possibly cursed by revealing one's name. So the most common way of describing oneself is as the "son of so-and-so" or the mother of (your youngest child).

11. Novak, op. cit., 39.

12. Ibid., 39.

13. Eugene Fisher, op. cit., 9.

14. Ray S. Anderson and Dennis B. Guernsey, *On Being Human* (Grand Rapids, Mich.: Eerdmans, 1985), 123-124.

15. Laurens van der Post, *The Lost World of the Kalahari* (London: Penguin Books, 1958), 235.

Chapter Five/Family Feud

1. Some of this chapter is adapted from R. Paul Stevens, "Family Feud: A Close Look at Genesis 25-35," *His* (December 1981), 18-20.

2. Kenneth Leech, *Experiencing God: Theology as Spirituality* (New York: Harper and Row, 1985), 67, emphasis mine. Leech further comments, "To neglect the Old Testament and the historical revelation is thus to fall prey to an idealist notion of God as pure spirit, a reversal to paganism. Today's 'Christian paganism,' abandoning its Jewish insights of materialism and historicity, offers religion as an integrating process, a civic cement, a protection against disturbance. In so doing, it protects itself against the disruptive, disturbing God of Jewish and Christian history."

3. It is sometimes noted that "Jacob" can also have a positive meaning: "God is my rear-guard," or "the Lord is at my heels." Perhaps his mother crafted this double-entente. In any event, Jacob chose to live out the sinister possibility of his own name.

4. Arthur Miller, *Death of a Salesman* (New York: Viking Press, 1949), quoted in William Hulme, *Living with Myself* (Minneapolis: Augsburg Publishing House, 1971), 69.

5. R. D. Laing, op. cit., 81.

6. Eugene Lowry, *The Homiletical Plot* (Atlanta: John Knox Press, 1980), 55.

7. Frank Boreham, *The Prodigal* (London: Epworth Press, n.d.), 32-33.

8. *Die last tragt mich*, quoted in Helmut Thielicke, *Und Wenn Gott Ware* (Qwee Verlag Stuttgart, 1970), 238.

9. Leech, *Experiencing God*, op. cit., 65.

10. Michael Novak, op. cit., 40.

11. James S. Stewart, *A Faith to Proclaim* (London: Hodder and Stoughton, 1953), 40.

Chapter Six/Raising Godly Parents

1. Quoted in F. E. Keelett, "Family Spirituality," in Gordon S. Wakefield, ed., *The Westminster Dictionary of Christian Spirituality* (Philadelphia: Westminster Press, 1983), 145.

2. *Apostolicam Actuositatem*, art. 11; see *Gaudium et Spes*, arts, 47-52.

3. Frederick J. Parella, "Towards a Spirituality of the Family," *Communio*, Vol. 9 (Summer 1982), 127-141.

4. Ibid., 135.

5. Martin Luther, "The Estate of Marriage," Walther I. Brandt, ed. and trans., *Luther's Works* (Philadelphia: Fortress Press, 1962), 40.

6. I first encountered the profound significance of leaving, cleaving, and one flesh in covenant-formation in Walter Trobish's *I Married You*, and I have developed

this in *Getting Ready for a Great Marriage* (NavPress) and *Married for Good* (Inter-Varsity Press).

7. See "*Paideia*," Colin Brown, ed., *The New International Dictionary of New Testament Theology*, vol. 3 (Grand Rapids, Mich.: Zondervan, 1978), 775-780. Typical of this fine article are these words: "But it is always God, not the child, or an ideal, who is central and forms its content. The educational aim of God is to lead his people to the realization that they owe their existence to the saving will of Yahweh alone, and therefore owe obedience to their divine instructor (Deut. 8:1-6)" (p. 777).

8. Henri Nouwen, *Reaching Out: Three Movements of the Spiritual Life* (Garden City, N.Y.: Doubleday and Co., 1975), 56.

9. Ibid., 57.

10. Anderson and Guernsey, op. cit., 136.

Chapter Seven/Contemplative Sexuality

1. The definitive piece of scholarship on this text is Phyllis A. Bird, "Male and Female He Created Them: Gen. 1:27b in the Context of the Priestly Account of Creation," *The Harvard Theological Review* 74:2 (1981), 129-139. The gist of her linguistic analysis is that the parallel coda (in the image of God he created him/male and female he created them) is progressive and not synonymous. She argues convincingly that the specification of humanity's bisexual nature is dictated by the larger structure of the chapter. Therefore she concludes that the first meaning of "male and female" is not a reference to the relational nature of the image of God but to fertility. Bird's analysis surprisingly ends up supporting the view of Dietrich Bonhoeffer, expanded by Karl Barth and many modern scholars, that the image of God is relational, and that both sexes are required for God's full representation to be made in the human race.

2. Much of this chapter was first published in my article, "Breaking the Gender Impasse," *Christianity Today* (January 13, 1992), 28-31.

3. Susan Foh shows conclusively that the etymology of the word *desire* in Genesis 3:16 supports a nonsexual understanding of the word, similar to its use in 4:7 for the desire of sin to overmaster Cain. Men rule; women revolt. Both are the result of sin. Susan T. Foh, *Women and the Word of God: A Response to Biblical Feminism*, (Phillipsburg, N.J.: Presbyterian and Reformed Publishing Co., 1979), 66-69. Bruce Waltke supports Foh's interpretation by offering two further lines of evidence: Bruce Waltke, "The Relationship of the Sexes in the Bible," *Crux*, vol. XIX, no. 3 (September 1983), 14.

4. These points and the one that follow are more fully developed with scholarly citations in my article: "The Mystery of Male and Female: Biblical and Trinitarian Models," *Themelios*, vol. 17, no. 3 (April/May 1992), 20-24.

5. Jean Vanier, *Man and Woman He Made Them*, (Toronto, Ont.: Anglican Book Centre, 1985), 50. The seeming anatomical justification of the double standard (that a man may have sex with several partners, since he is not marked by the encounter, but a woman may not, because she has allowed a man to come inside her and so is indelibly marked) is not supported by Scripture. This is carefully considered by Helmut Thielicke, "The Mystery of Sexuality," in *Are You Nobody?* (Richmond: John Knox Press, 1965), 45-60.

6. See especially Gordon Fee's treatment of the Corinthian passages in *The First Epistle to the Corinthians*, op. cit., 498-530, 699-713, and John Nolland, in *Crux*, vol. XIX, no. 3 (September 1983) on 1 Timothy 2. It appears that 1 Corinthians 11 deals with relationships, not ministry, on the assumption made by some Corinthian women that since the end had come sexual differences were meaningless. Paul

repudiates this eschatological breaking down of sexes, as he would repudiate androgyny today. 1 Corinthians 11:2-3 does not teach a chain-of-command, but male-female relationships that resemble God-Christ. 1 Corinthians 14:34-38 is textually the most difficult of the three, as it seems to contradict Paul's clear teaching in 1 Corinthians 11:10 that a woman has her own authority *(exousia)* to minister in prayer or prophecy when she is in right relationship to men. Judging the passage in 14:34-38 as non-Pauline appears to me unwarranted, so we are left making a sanctified guess: Was Paul forbidding women to evaluate prophecies in public, a role normally assigned to elders? 1 Timothy 2:8-15 addresses an ad hoc situation in which false teachers (2 Tim. 3:6) had doctrinally seduced the women, making it a replay of the Garden scene (1 Tim. 2:14). Here Paul shuts down women's ministry completely (2:12) using, once again, a creational argument (2:13). All three of these passages have been weighted disproportionately, especially in the light of the example of Jesus in relation to women, a fundamental truth usually ignored.

7. See the chapter "The Problem of Headship," in *Married for Good* (Downers Grove, Ill.: InterVarsity Press, 1986) and "Mutual Submission: Reversing the Curse," in *Marriage Spirituality* (Downers Grove, Ill.: InterVarsity Press, 1989).

8. See David Jeffrey's splendid treatment of the linguistic basis of God as Father as a response to the *Inclusive Language Lectionary: A companion work under the National Council of Churches to the RSV revision:* David Lyle Jeffrey, "Inclusivity and Our Language of Worship," in *The Reformed Journal* (August 1987), 13-22.

9. J. I. Packer, "God," in Ferguson, Wright and Packer, eds., *The New Dictionary of Theology* (Downers Grove, Ill.: InterVarsity Press, 1988), 274-277.

10. Tomas Spidlik, *The Spirituality of the Christian East: A Systematic Handbook* (Kalamazoo, Mich.: Cistercian Publications, 1986), 45.

11. Dr. James Houston argues that "to all intents and purposes, Augustine states that the relations within the godhead are irrelevant to their being God. . . . It is as if God is God, in spite of the Trinity!" In contrast to this the Greek Fathers insisted that God's relations with man are internal to God's own character. In harmony with this, Dr. Houston traces the fact that in Western spirituality there has been a renewed mysticism (a direct personal experience of the presence of God) whenever there was contact with the trinitarian insights of the Greek Fathers. Trinitarian faith invites and evokes relationship (James Houston, "Trinitarian Spirituality," unpublished [Vancouver, B.C.: Regent College, 1989).

12. Ibid.

Chapter Eight/Full Partnership in Ministry

1. From *Perelandra* or *Voyage to Venus* (London: Pan Books, 1983).

2. Cited in Janet Moreley, "In God's Image?" *New Blackfriars* 63.747 (1982), 375, quoted in Kenneth Leech, *Experiencing God*, op. cit., 374.

3. This imaginary interview was first published in my article, "The Mystery of Male and Female: Biblical and Trinitarian Models," op. cit., 20-24.

4. R. Paul Stevens, *Liberating the Laity* (Downers Grove, Ill.: InterVarsity Press, 1985), 33. See also my thoughts (pp. 109-124) on the process of liberating women for ministry in Marineview Chapel at that time, a process that has led subsequently to the appointment of women elders and preachers in University Chapel.

5. This is the phrase I use in *The Equipper's Guide to Every Member Ministry* (Downers Grove, Ill.: InterVarsity, 1992). In a further volume Phil Collins and I explore a systemic approach to equipping that bears directly on our subject. Men and women are interdependent in the church system, and change in one requires

change in the other. See *The Equipping Pastor: A Systems Approach to Congregational Leadership* (Washington, D.C.: An Alban Institute Publication, forthcoming).

6. Hendrik Kraemer, *A Theology of the Laity* (Philadelphia: Westminster Press, 1958), 70.

7. Michael Griffiths, "Leadership," in Alan Bamford, ed., *Where Do We Go From Here?* (Worthing: H. E. Walter Ltd., 1979), 22.

8. Quoted in Michael Griffiths, "Maturity," in Allan Bamford, ed., op. cit., 77.

9. It is seldom noticed that the only text in the New Testament where we are told how husbands and wives are to make decisions (1 Cor. 7:5) pleads for *mutual consent!*

10. James B. Hurley, *Man and Woman in Biblical Perspective* (Grand Rapids, Mich.: Zondervan, 1981), 202-204. Hurley rejects, rightly, the cultural argument but fails to deal with the textual meaning of *authentein*, though he admits in a footnote he is waiting for published research on that unusual word.

11. O. Betz, "Might," in Colin Brown, ed., *The New International Dictionary of New Testament Theology*, op. cit., vol. 2, 611.

12. Paul's greetings refer to nineteen men and ten women known to him, all of them endowed with spiritual gifts by the Holy Spirit. Tryphena and Tryphosa (Dainty and Delicate) and Persis are all said to "labor in the Lord" a favorite Pauline word for the Christian ministry. Junia could either be a common female name, or a shortened form of a less common male name Junias. At least one fourth-century commentator (Chrysostom) believed that Junia was a female apostle. Phoebe was not only called deacon (masculine—quite probably an officer) but *prostatis*, a word which means "protectress," "patroness," or "helper." It is important not to let our imaginations "fly" with these statements. It can at least be said that women played a key role in the early church and it is hard to imagine that when "leading women" followed Paul (Acts 17:4, 12) they adopted silence and ceased to give some kind of leadership.

13. Jean Vanier, *Man and Woman He Made Them* (Toronto, Ont.: Anglican Book Centre, 1985), 54.

14. Ray S. Anderson offers a helpful perspective on this: While we honestly lack historical precedents for the full liberation of women into partnership in church leadership, we are not lacking in eschatological precedents. We know what the primitive church did under the Lordship of Christ in its own day. We also know that the primitive church was not able fully to experience the truth preached by the apostles. "The resurrection of Jesus to be the living Lord constitutes a continuing hermeneutical criterion of the church's understanding of itself as under the authority of Scripture" (Ray S. Anderson, "The Resurrection of Jesus as a Hermeneutic Criterion, Pt. 1," in *TSF Bulletin*, vol. 9, no. 3 (January-February 1986), 10.

15. Ray S. Anderson, "The Resurrection of Jesus as a Hermeneutic Criterion, Pt. 2," in *TSF Bulletin*, vol. 9, no. 4 (March/April 1986), 16.

Chapter Nine/Prayer and Sexuality

1. Neoplatonism has been the underlying philosophy of most of the history of the Western church. William J. Rademacher in *Lay Ministry: A Theological, Spiritual and Pastoral Handbook* (New York: Crossroad, 1991), writing from the Catholic viewpoint, shows conclusively that the Catholic defense of celibacy as a superior way does not come from Scripture, as is currently being argued, but from the underlying Neoplatonism that the church absorbed from the Greek world.

2. I acknowledge my indebtedness for this thought to Dr. Robert Banks, who graciously read the manuscript and made many helpful suggestions.

3. Mike Mason, *The Mystery of Marriage* (Portland, Oreg.: Multnomah Press, 1985), 81.

4. Quoted in Richard Mouw, *Called to Holy Worldliness* (Philadelphia: Fortress Press, 1980), 111-112.

5. It is also seldom noted that "be filled with the Spirit" is a *plural* imperative addressed not to the solitary individual but to people in community.

6. Mason, op. cit., 8.

7. This is Dr. Luke's special contribution to the vexed divorce question. He sandwiched the divorce teaching of Jesus (Luke 16:18) between two parables that have to do with our readiness to hear the voice of God. In the second parable—about the rich man and Lazarus—Jesus puts into the mouth of Abraham his own words of frustration: "If they do not listen to Moses and the Prophets, they will not be convinced even if someone (like me) rises from the dead" (16:31). The teaching on the divorceless covenant (16:18) is the Lord's example from the Law and the Prophets. The implication of the chapter taken as a whole is this: If we ignore a word from God, for example on the unconditional permanent nature of the marriage covenant, we will gradually harden our hearts and close our ears to other words from God. Even a resurrection—or some other sign or wonder—will not convince people who refuse the word they already have. I admit there are many pastoral questions surrounding the teaching of Jesus about divorce and the church must be compassionate toward those who have suffered a marriage breakdown. But the text *in this case* is concerned with what easy divorce and inevitable remarriage will do to our spirituality.

8. In contrast to this, John Chrysostom, the golden-tongued preacher of the fourth century, complained that the angel's life for which we should strive cannot be found in marriage: "When a married man comes home he must look after his wife and take care of many things which a single man does not have to bother with. This is certainly the case if his wife is beautiful and attractive; but if she is a real shrew, then his presence in the house is more in the nature of a punishment from heaven. How can the man who is weighed down by worldly cares, bound by so many fetters and constantly chained to an ill-tempered wife, scale the heights of heaven?" (St. John Chrysostom, *De Virg.*, XLIV, PS 48, 566-567, quoted in Alfons Auer, op. cit., 32.

9. Dolores Leckey, op. cit., 17.

10. R. Paul Stevens, *Marriage Spirituality: Ten Disciplines for Couples Who Love God* (Downers Grove, Ill.: InterVarsity Press, 1989), 60.

11. Richard Rohr, op. cit., 30.

12. Brook B. Herbert, "Prayer and Sexuality" (unpublished paper for Biblical Spirituality 580 [April 1991], Vancouver, B.C.: Regent College), 9.

13. Ibid., 10-11. It is a privilege to receive such a thoughtful and mature submission from a student. In the royal priesthood teachers are co-learners!

14. 1 Samuel 18:1-4; 19:1-4; 20:17, 42; 23:16.

Chapter Ten/Relational Spirituality

1. R. D. Laing, op. cit., 50.

2. Ibid., 62.

3. Simone Weil, *Waiting on God* (London: Fontana, 1950), 157.

4. Ibid., 157.

5. Aelred of Rievaulx, *Spiritual Friendship*, Mary Eugenis Laker, trans. (Kalamazoo, Mich.: Cistercian Publications, 1974), 63.

6. Unfortunately Aelred's writings—*Mirror of Charity* (1140) and *Spiritual Friendship* (1160)—are tainted with Neoplatonism. He envisioned a continuous movement

from physical loves to pure love of God, from lower friendships to pure spiritual friendships that take us to the heart of God.

7. Ibid., 60.

8. James Houston, *Transforming Friendship* (Oxford: Lion, 1989), 195-196.

9. Dietrich Bonhoeffer. *The Cost of Discipleship* (London: SCM Press, 1959), 85-88.

10. Blaise Pascal, *Pensées* (New York: The Modern Library, 1941), 166, quoted in Eugene H. Peterson, *Reversed Thunder: The Revelation of John and the Praying Imagination* (Cambridge: Harper and Row, 1988), 95.

11. Quoted in Peterson, op. cit., 87.

12. Howard A. Snyder, *The Radical Wesley and Patterns for Church Renewal* (Downers Grove, Ill.: InterVarsity Press, 1980), 60.

13. Bonheoffer, *Life Together*, op. cit., 110.

14. F. Kefa Sempangi, "Walking in the Light," *Sojourners* (February 1978), 27.

Chapter Eleven/Mutuality

1. Markus Barth. *Ephesians Translation and Commentary on Chapters 4-6*, vol. 34a, in *The Anchor Bible* (Garden City, N.Y.:, Doubleday, 1981), 449.

2. An encouraging example of this took place in the ministry of Davida Foy Crabtree in the Colchester Federated Church, where she was the pastor. She used listening groups to visit members and inquire how their faith relates to their daily work. The pastor was part of this but she had taken the vow of silence! (Davida Foy Crabtree, *The Empowering Church: How One Congregation Supports Lay People's Ministries in the World* [Washington, D.C.: An Alban Institute Publication, 1989]).

Chapter Twelve/Embodied Love

1. In reality Christian priesthood has three objects: people, the world, and God.

2. Quoted in Roland Bainton, *Here I Stand* (New York: Mentor Books, 1950), 181.

3. I acknowledge my indebtedness for part of the following outline to Robert Farrar Capon in *An Offering of Uncles: The Priesthood of Adam and the Shape of the World* (New York: Crossroad, 1982), 18-28.

4. Ibid., 26-28.

5. A remarkable example of how an ordinary couple was able to make a difference in creating "place" in the City of Pasadena is told in Basil Entwisle, *Making Cities Work: How Two People Mobilized a Community to Meet Its Needs* (Pasadena, Calif.: Hope Publishing House, 1990).

6. Recent scholarship has called into question this stark contrast of *chronos* and *kairos* by showing that the words are sometimes used interchangeably. The textual use of these may not yield as strong a contrast as I have made here, though the distinction stands in our experience of time.

7. Madeleine L'Engle, *Walking on Water: Reflections on Faith and Art* (Wheaton Ill.: Shaw Publishers, 1980), 98.

8. Capon, op. cit., 163. A remarkable commentary on the book of Job comes to the same conclusion: there is something more important than getting an answer to our questions about the problem of pain—the contemplation of God (Gustavo Gutierrez, *On Job: God-talk and the Suffering of the Innocent*, Matthew J. O'Connell, trans. [Maryknoll, N.Y.: Orbis Books, 1987], 14).

Chapter Thirteen/Disciplines of the Hungry Heart

1. Von Hugel, *The Mystical Element of Religion*, II, 127, quoted in Auer, op. cit., 72.

2. Richard Pollay, "The Distorted Mirror: Reflections on the Unintended Consequences of Advertising," Working Paper No. 1005, History of Advertising Archives, University of British Columbia, 4.

3. Chaim Potok, *The Chosen* (Greenwich, Conn.: Fawcett Publications, 1967), 265.

4. See Henri Nouwen's treatment of the spiritual movement from loneliness to solitude in Nouwen, op. cit., 14-44.

5. William E. Collins, "A Sermon from Hell: Toward a Theology of Loneliness," *Journal of Religion and Health*, vol. 28, no. 1, Spring 1989, 76.

6. Ibid., 74.

7. John Calvin, *Institutes of the Christian Religion*, III, xx. 28, quoted in Don Postema, *Space for God: The Study and Practice of Prayer and Spirituality* (Grand Rapids, Mich.: Bible Way, 1983), 68.

8. Oswald Chambers, *My Utmost for His Highest* (New York: Dodd, Mead and Co., 1956), 291.

9. Blaise Pascal, *Pensées*, 525-526.

10. A very useful meditation based on the Ten Commandments was crafted by Walter Trobish. *The Questionnaire of God* is available from Editions Trobish, Lange Strasse 50, D-7570 Baden-Baden, Germany.

11. Quoted in Name Withheld, "The War Within: An Anatomy of Lust," *Leadership* (Fall, 1982), 45.

12. St. John Chrysostom, *On Wealth and Poverty*, Catherine P. Roth, trans. (Crestwood, N.Y.: St. Valdimir's Seminary Press, 1984), 59.

13. McCheyne's Calendar for Daily Readings, obtainable from The Banner of Truth Trust, P.O. Box 621, Carlisle, Penn., 17013, U.S.A. This lectionary takes one through the Old Testament once a year, and the New Testament and Psalms twice a year.

14. James Houston, "The Act of Bible Reading: Towards a Biblical Spirituality," Elmer Dyck, ed., *How Shall We Then Read?* (Downers Grove: InterVarsity Press, forthcoming), 4.

15. See *A Manual of Catholic Devotion* (London, 1969) and Anthony de Mello, *Sadhana: A Way to God* (Anand, India, 1978).

16. Other Scriptures that easily lend themselves to meditation are Psalms 1, 63, 73, 139; Matthew 13:44, 46; John 15:1-17; 2 Corinthians 5:15-21; 3:16-18; Hebrews 11; Hosea 2:14-23; Mark 11:22-26; Ephesians 3:14-21; Revelation 3:19-20; 1 John 3:1; Luke 11:1-14; Isaiah 66:1-2; Luke 7:35-36; Song of Songs 4:10-15; 1 Kings 19:1-18; 1 Samuel 3; Matthew 13:9-17; Isaiah 48:12-19.

17. A.W. Tozer, *The Pursuit of God* (Harrisburg: Christian Publications, 1948), 14, quoted in Walter Hilton, *Toward a Perfect Love*, David L. Jeffrey, trans., op. cit., xxviii.

Chapter Fourteen/The Journey Inward

1. Quoted in Morton Kelsey, *Encounter with God: A Theology of Christian Experience* (London: Hodder and Stoughton, 1974), 181-182.

2. E. Stanley Jones, *Conversion* (Nashville, Tenn.: Abingdon Press, 1959), 210.

3. Ibid., 214.

Chapter Fifteen/Becoming Real

1. Madeleine L'Engle, *The Weather of the Heart* (Wheaton, Ill.: Harold Shaw, 1978), 84-85.

2. Walter of Hilton, op. cit., 91-92.

3. Margery Williams, *The Velveteen Rabbit* (London: William Heinemann Ltd., 1978), 8-10.

Chapter Sixteen/The Poor

1. Ivan Head, "Why should we care about the Third World?" *The Globe and Mail* (Toronto: August 24, 1991), D5.
2. Clark H. Pinnock, "An Evangelical Theology of Human Liberation," *Sojourners* (February 1976), quoted in Ronald J. Sider, *Rich Christians in an Age of Hunger* (Downers Grove, Ill.: InterVarsity Press, 1977), 77.
3. St. John Chrysostom, op. cit., 47.
4. Ibid., 47.
5. Ibid., 50.
6. Ibid., 49.
7. Ibid., 57.
8. Ibid., 55, emphasis mine.
9. In trying to understand how ministry to the poor can be simultaneously ministry to Jesus we may follow several lines of thought: (1) In both the Old Testament (Prov. 19:17; Ps. 140:12; Deut. 26:5-8) and the New (James 2:5; Matt. 25:35-40) God shows preferential love for the poor and powerless; (2) in his own Incarnation, the Son of God chose to take the lowest place in the human family (Phil. 2:8); (3) the gospel itself means release to the captives and good news to the poor (Luke 4:18-19) and therefore as the poor hear that Good News we should expect to meet Jesus and be met by Him; (4) there is the direct word of Jesus in Matt. 25:35 that he is present. I do not think it is necessary to argue that Jesus lives in the poor. Rather, he *meets us* when we love the poor and powerless. See Sider, op. cit.
10. Quoted in Jean Vanier, *Male and Female,* op. cit., 173.
11. The name Lazarus means "God is my helper," a detail that would have been obvious to the first hearers of the parable. Unlike the rich, who are self-sufficient, Lazarus looked to God.

Chapter Seventeen/The Stranger

1. Nouwen, op. cit., 50-51.
2. Ibid., 51.
3. Elizabeth O'Connor, *Eighth Day of Creation* (Waco, Tex.: Word, 1971), 13.
4. Ibid., 10, emphasis mine.
5. Chrysostom, op. cit., 50-51.

Chapter Eighteen/The Outsider

1. Quoted in Kraemer, op. cit., 175.
2. Quoted in Robert Raines, *Creative Brooding* (New York: Macmillan Co., 1966), 51.

Chapter Nineteen/The Compulsive Pursuit of Leisure

1. "How America Has Run Out of Time," *Time* (April 24, 1989), 48-55.
2. "In 1967 testimony before a Senate subcommittee indicated that by 1985 people would be working just 22 hours a week or could retire at 38," ibid., 49.
3. This information is attributed to Peter Eicher, "The Age of Freedom: A Christian Community for Leisure and the World of Work," Robert Nowell, trans., in *At One Time and in One Place.*
4. *Time,* op. cit., 50.
5. Peter Eicher, op. cit., 44.
6. *Time,* op. cit., 50.

7. Quoted in Robert K. Johnston, *The Christian at Play* (Grand Rapids, Mich.: Eerdmans, 1983), 11.

8. Gordon Macdonald, *Ordering Your Private World* (Nashville: Nelson, 1984), 45-47.

9. Ibid., 48.

10. Leech, *True Prayer*, op. cit., 60.

Chapter Twenty/Playing Heaven

1. Dr. Robert Banks suggests that the leisure industry reinterprets vocation as vacation!

2. There are, however, a score of books that deal with something loosely called "a theology of leisure": Paul A. Heintzman, *A Christian Perspective on the Philosophy of Leisure* (Ottawa: National Library of Canada, 1985); Robert K. Johnston, *The Christian At Play* (Grand Rapids, Mich.: Eerdmans, 1983); John Oswalt, *The Leisure Crisis: A Biblical Perspective on Guilt-Free Leisure* (Wheaton, Ill.: Victor Books, 1987); Leland Ryken, *Work and Leisure in Christian Perspective* (Portland, Oreg.: Multnomah Press, 1987).

3. Gustavo Gutiérrez, *On Job: God-Talk and the Suffering of the Innocent* (Maryknoll, N.Y.: Orbid Books, 1988), 75. Gutiérrez makes the remarkable statement that there is something more important than getting justice: the contemplation of God himself!

4. See the chapter "Sabbath: Playing Heaven Together," in *Marriage Spirituality* op. cit., 53-68.

5. Robert K. Johnston, op. cit., 14, suggests that even married couples have joined the "harried leisure class" by devoting less and less time to making love. He quotes Staffen B. Linder, author of *The Harried Leisure Class*, with these words: "People have not stopped making love any more than they have stopped eating. But—to extend the surprisingly adequate parallel with the joys of gastronomy—less time is devoted to both preparation and savouring. . . . A pleasure has turned into the satisfaction of a basic need—'a grocer's orgy'—a maintenance function—a conjugal duty" ([New York: Columbia University Press, 1970], 88).

6. Johnston, op. cit., 85. Remarkably, however, there is even in Puritan writings a strong sense of the importance of the balanced life. Richard Baxter in *Christian Ethics* advises, "If it be possible, choose a calling which so exerciseth the body, as not to overwhelm you with cares and labour, and deprive you of all leisure for the holy and noble employments of the mind; and which so exerciseth your mind, as to allow you some exercise for the body also" (*The Practical Works of Richard Baxter* [Ligonier, Penn.: Soli Deo Gloria Publications, 1990], vol. 1, 377).

7. Johnston, op. cit., 43.

8. Many of these thoughts were expressed first by me in "Sabbath: Playing Heaven Together" in *Marriage Spirituality*, 54-55.

9. In Hugh Rahner, *Man At Play* (New York: Herder and Herder, 1972), xvi.

10. Ibid., 42-43.

11. Ibid., 43.

12. William Diehl, *Thank God It's Monday* (Philadelphia: Fortress Press, 1982), 171.

13. Jurgen Moltmann, *God in Creation: An Ecological Doctrine of Creation*, Margaret Kohl, trans. (London: SCM, 1985), 287.

14. Ibid., 286, emphasis mine.

15. In the Syrian *Peshida* reflecting the Aramaic, Jesus is reported to say, "Come to me . . . and I will rest you . . . for I am restful. . . and you will find rest for yourselves."

16. Moltmann, op. cit., 286.

17. Loren Wilkinson, "Garden-City-Sabbath: Hints Toward A Theology of Culture," unpublished (Vancouver, B.C.: Regent College, 1989).

Chapter Twenty-One/Reinventing Sabbath

1. See Alan D. Goldman, "The Sabbath as Dialectic: Implications for Mental Health," *Journal of Religion and Health* 25:3 (Fall 1986), 237-244.

2. Quoted in Timothy Ware, *The Orthodox Church* (Harmondsworth, England: Penguin Books, 1988), 269.

3. Heschel quotes a remarkably similar saying of the rabbis: "The Sabbath is given unto you, not you unto the Sabbath" (Mekilta to 31:13, Quoted in Heschel, op. cit., 17).

4. See note 13, Chapter 13.

5. Robert Banks notes that verse 2 of Psalm 127—"In vain you rise early and stay up late, toiling for food to eat—for he grants sleep to those he loves"—exegetes verse 1—"Unless the Lord builds the house, its builders labor in vain." By having adequate sleep we demonstrate, as verse 2 shows, that we live by faith, not by works.

6. Brother Lawrence, *The Practice of the Presence of God* (Westwood, N.J.: Fleming Revell, 1958), 19.

7. Vincent van Gogh. *The Complete Letters of Vincent van Gogh* (Greenwich: New York Graphic Society), vol. 1, 197.

Epilogue: The Eighth Day of Creation

1. Barnabas 15:8-9, in *The Apostolic Fathers*, trans. Kirsopp Lake, vol. 1 (Cambridge, Mass.: Harvard University Press, 1975), 395-397. Emphasis mine.

2. Auer, op. cit., 156.

3. Robert A. Markus, "Work and Worker in Early Christianity" in John N. Todd, ed. *Work: Christian Thought and Practice* (Baltimore: Helicon Press, 1960) no page, in Davida Foy Crabtree, "Empowering the Ministry of the Laity in Workplace, Home and Community: A Programatic and Systemic Approach in the Local Church (unpublished D. Min. thesis for Hartford Seminary, 1989), 47.

4. Heschel, op. cit., 73.

5. Ibid., 74.

6. Ibid., 76.

7. Ibid., 75.

8. Ibid., 90-91.